# WRITING WAR

# WRITING WAR

## Fiction, Gender, and Memory

**LYNNE HANLEY**

The University of
Massachusetts Press
Amherst

Copyright © 1991 by
The University of Massachusetts Press
All rights reserved
Printed in the United States of America
LC 90–49252
ISBN 0–87023–738–1 (cloth); 748–9 (pbk.)
Designed by Dede Heath
Set in Linotron Electra by Keystone Typesetting, Inc.
Printed and bound by Thomson-Shore, Inc.

Library of Congress Cataloging-in-Publication Data

Hanley, Lynne, 1943–
    Writing war : fiction, gender, and memory / Lynne Hanley.
        p.   cm.
    Includes bibliographical references.
    ISBN 0–87023–738–1 (alk. paper). — ISBN 0–87023–748–9 (pbk. alk.
paper)
        1. War stories, English—Women authors—History and criticism.
    2. War stories, American—Women authors—History and criticism.
    3. Women and literature—Great Britain—History—20th century.
    4. Women and literature—United States—History—20th century.
    5. American fiction—20th century—History and criticism.   6. English
fiction—20th century—History and criticism.   7. Sex role in literature.
    8. War stories, American.   I. Title.
    PR888.W37H36   1991
    823'.9109358—dc20                                                90–49252
                                                                              CIP

British Library Cataloguing in Publication data are available.

Vera Brittain's poem, "We Shall Come No More," from her autobiography,
*Testament of Youth*, is included with the permission of Paul Berry, her literary
executor, Victor Gollancz Ltd., and Virago Press.

Excerpts from "Daddy," are from *Collected Poems of Sylvia Plath*, by Sylvia
Plath, published by Faber & Faber, London. Copyright © 1963, 1965, 1981
by Ted Hughes. Reprinted by permission of HarperCollins Publishers and
Olwyn Hughes.

For Bill and Jesse

The man, the woman, sitting humbly in the corner of their room, stare at that indescribably perfect thing, a golden chestnut leaf in autumn, when it has just floated down from the tree, and then may perform any one of a number of acts that rise from inside themselves, and that they could not justify nor argue with or against—they may simply close a hand over it, crushing it to powder, and fling the stuff out of the window, watching the dust sink through the air to the pavement, for there is a relief in thinking that the rains of next week will seep the leaf-stuff back through the soil to the roots, so that next year, at least, it will shine in the air again. Or the woman may bow before it, ironically, and with a sort of apology that is so near to the thoughts and actions of Shikastans now, and think that the laws that made this shape must be, must be, must be stronger in the end than the slow distorters and perverters of the substance of life. Or the man, glancing out of the window, forcing himself to see the tree in its other truth, that of the fierce and furious war of eating and being eaten, may see suddenly, for an instant, so that it has gone even as he turns to call his wife: Look, look, quick!— behind the seethe and scramble and eating that is one truth, and behind the ordinary tree-in-autumn that is the other—a third, a tree of a fine, high, shimmering light, like shaped sunlight. A world, a world, another world, another truth. . . .

And when the dark comes, he will look up and out and see a little smudge of light that is a galaxy that exploded millions of years ago, and the oppression that had gripped his heart lifts, and he laughs, and he calls his wife and says: Look, we are seeing something that ceased to exist millions of years ago—and she sees, exactly, and laughs with him.

Doris Lessing, *Shikasta*

# Contents

# Acknowledgments

For their encouragement, support, and good advice, I wish to thank Margaret Cerullo, Elly Donkin, Mel Heath, Manda Heron, Paul Jenkins, Marjorie Kaufman, Jill Lewis, Anne Mellor, Nina Payne, Bill Quillian, Fred Robinson, Will Ryan, Ellie Siegel, Claire Sprague, Jean Sudrann, Judith Wilt, and my editor, Pam Wilkinson.

"War Stories," "To El Salvador," and an earlier version of "Virginia Woolf and the Romance of Oxbridge" are reprinted from the *Massachusetts Review,* © 1983, 1985, 1987, The Massachusetts Review, Inc. An earlier version of "The War Zone" also appeared in the same journal in 1989 under the title "Thinking Bayonets."

Portions of "Reconstructing Vietnam" and "War and Postmodern Memory" first appeared in *Radical America* as "The Official Story: Imagining Vietnam" and "Her Story of War: Demilitarizing Literature and Literary Studies."

"Little Women" was first printed in *Sojourner: The Women's Forum* 4, no. 1 (1988).

# WRITING WAR

# Introduction

Having recently read *The War of the Worlds*, I am reminded of the power of fiction to create memory. I know perfectly well I have never seen a Martian, just as I know I have never experienced the terrors of an invasion of my neighborhood by creatures both invincible and utterly alien, yet I now have in mind a distinct and detailed account of these events, which, when summoned, particularly after a lapse of time, has the character of a memory of a lived experience. I can, of course, normally distinguish between my memories of characters and events in books and my memories of people and events in my life, but in memory they have a similar presence, a like authority.

In a conversation at a party not long ago, I was trying to recall the history of Mr. Bulstrode, the crooked banker in George Eliot's *Middlemarch*. My effort to recollect the exact details of his wrongdoing seemed suddenly like an effort to recall some old grievance of my own against a person I hadn't seen or thought of in years. And, indeed, later that evening, someone mentioned the name of a woman I hadn't liked in college or heard of since, and when I recalled this woman, she had the same presence in my mind as Bulstrode, as though, over time, Bulstrode had gained in actuality what my college acquaintance had lost to fiction.

My point is that our fictions have power, they shape our memories of the past and they create memories of pasts we have never had, of experiences not even remotely like anything that has ever happened to us. And these narratives of exotic experience may have the most power over us of all, because we can't challenge their authenticity with the evidence of our own senses. We can't say to H. G. Wells, "No, it wasn't like that when Martians landed in my backyard."

Most Americans living in this decade have not directly experienced war, have not fought at the front, or been invaded, occupied, or bombed at home, so our narratives of war are particularly potent in shaping our imagination, indeed our very memory, of war. And since how we imagine (or remember, or forget) war has a great deal to do with our propensity to make war, the question occurs, What is it in our literature of war, in our modern cultural memory of war, that has led us in this century to make war again and again, and to export our organized violence to just about every corner of the world?

In her recent collection of essays, *Prisons We Choose to Live Inside*, Doris Lessing writes:

> I think it is sentimental to discuss the subject of war, or peace, without acknowledging that a great many people enjoy war—not only the idea of it, but the fighting itself. In my time I have sat through many many hours listening to people talking about war, the prevention of war, the awfulness of war, with it never once being mentioned that for large numbers of people the idea of war is exciting, and that when a war is over they may say it was the best time in their lives. This may be true even of people whose experiences in war were terrible, and which ruined their lives. People who have lived through a war know that as it approaches, an at first secret, unacknowledged elation begins, as if an almost inaudible drum is beating . . . an awful, illicit, violent excitement is abroad. Then the elation becomes too strong to be ignored or overlooked: then everyone is possessed by it.[1]

Our war literature of this century, or at least that selection of it that we have come to know as our literature on the subject, is permeated, I think, with this "secret, unacknowledged elation" at the thought of war, with the conviction that war is exciting and that soldiers experience in combat uniquely profound and intense emotions and relationships. Initially, I was shocked at the title of the 1984 *Esquire* article by William Broyles, Jr., "Why Men Love War," but then I was glad to see the cat out of the bag. As Lessing insists in *Prisons We Choose to Live Inside*, some people in every society enjoy thuggery, and war brings these people out, encourages them to indulge brutal and violent impulses that, in times of peace, they are obliged to keep under lock and key.

Certainly most popular representations in the United States of war, particularly since the onset of the Reagan years, make war look like a lot of fun. G.I. Joe toys have staged a remarkable comeback from their long decline since the late sixties; the invasions of Grenada and Panama looked on TV more like war camp than warfare; a recent issue of a local newspaper invited its readers to enjoy "Twenty-three hours in Jamaica with Westover's 439 Military Airlift Wing";[2] Oliver North is still grinning and still not in jail; and even "serious" films about real wars like *Platoon* or *Apocalypse Now* make the experience and emotions of American soldiers bigger and more important and more intense than those of anybody else. After World War I, Vera Brittain concluded that the glamorization of war—the "incomparable keying up of the spirit in a time of mortal conflict"[3] is the pacifist's real problem, yet both our popular and our highbrow representations of war sizzle with these keyed up emotions and yearn for the occasion of their release.

The act itself of writing about war no doubt misrepresents war by promoting a false sense of security. If the work is a memoir, the author has survived, and whether the work is autobiographical or the purest fiction, the reader's life is rarely on the line. However vivid and gripping the account, a reader's experience of war will never include one of war's most definitive emotions: the immediate and entirely legitimate fear of losing one's life, limbs, or senses, or of seeing the person next to one lose his. The reader who thinks literature imparts the truth about war will always discover that war is worse than he or she thinks, simply because one thing war is not, is settling down in an easy chair with a good book.

But war is subject to more deliberate misrepresentations than those that inhere in the form of the memoir or the situation of the reader. In my effort to give definition to the kind of memory our literature perpetuates of this century's many, many wars, I was naturally drawn to Paul Fussell's *The Great War and Modern Memory*. "The War Zone," the essay that opens this collection, is a critique of the memory of World War I Fussell constructs through his selection and interpretation of a particular body of literature. Though critics have challenged Fussell's estimate and analysis of particular writers and works, few have seriously questioned his canon of war literature or analyzed the emotions with which both the literature and Fussell's critical response to it are imbued. Though Sandra Gilbert, in a 1983 article in *Signs*, documented the enormous range and volume of women's literary production during and shortly after World War I,[4] for the most part Fussell's premise that war literature is by and about men at the front remains the operative premise in our identification of what poems, memoirs, and fictions constitute our literature on war. And since soldiers write our story of war, theirs is the perspective that prevails.

The next critical essay in this collection looks at the experience and the stance of a woman writer who did claim authorship in this very male, very military, and very narrowly defined terrain. The essay on Virginia Woolf traces her slow but relentless disillusionment with English culture, largely as a result of her increasingly imperative awareness that the procession of educated English gentlemen is leading, and has led, to war. "To El Salvador," the essay on Joan Didion, explores both the reluctance of the woman writer to face war—to relinquish the privilege she enjoys of disassociation from war—and the disillusionment that ensues when a woman recognizes in the man who makes war a man she knows, a husband, brother, or lover.

As the essay on Fussell points out, our war literature is obsessed with the experience of a very small portion of the large populations implicated in modern warfare. Over and over again, we hear the story of the white English or American soldier, as though his was the only real human presence on the field of war. And this story is almost always told by the soldier himself, and thus tends to plead his case. "Reconstructing Vietnam" looks at some of the implications of the authorship and content of the narrative that has come to be our dominant story of Vietnam, and the essay details the efforts by Joan Didion in *Democracy* and Doris Lessing in *Shikasta* to disrupt and reinscribe this narrative.

The final essay, "War and Postmodern Memory," explores the positioning of the woman writer in relation to the subject of war, and some of the exclusions, contradictions, and impositions to which she is subject. Since women are presumed to be absent from war, they are presumed to have no story to tell. The only woman who can claim authority to speak about war is the rare woman who has been at least near the combat zone, the odd nurse or motorcycle corps volunteer. Didion makes a radical response to this rite of passage when she chooses to go to the war in El Salvador. Doris Lessing makes a radical response of a different kind when she brings the combat zone home, when she defines the locus of bellicosity not as a place, a field of battle, but as a habit of mind, a structure of feeling, a cultural predisposition. In an interview with Roy Newquist a quarter of a century ago, Doris Lessing explained that the idea of her *Children of Violence* series was "to write about people like myself, people my age who are born out of wars and who have lived through them, the framework of lives in conflict."[5] *Children of Violence* enacts bellicosity as a deep-rooted structure of English consciousness, a structure asserted overtly in war but insinuated into all aspects of English culture: into relations between men and women and parents and children, into relations between people of different races, classes, religions, and nations. "War and Postmodern Memory" concludes with an exploration of Lessing's attempt, in *The Marriages between Zones Three, Four, and Five*, to reconstruct this fundamental bellicosity of English and American patriarchal consciousness.

As a structure of consciousness, bellicosity describes a mental habit of creating arbitrary categories that are presumed to be mutually exclusive and hostile (self/other, masculine/feminine, white/black, us/them), and of then insisting on the supremacy of one category over the other. For Virginia Woolf, this habit of mind is epitomized by "the monstrous male . . . scoring the floor of the earth with chalk marks, within whose mystic boundaries human beings are penned, rigidly, separately, artificially."[6] Since the assertion of the supremacy of one category over another requires, above all, an inflexible definition of membership, the bellicose mind is always resistant to any erosion of its "mystic boundaries."

As steeped in bellicosity as our culture is, it is not surprising that it should pervade what we like to think of as the humane world of literature. In the formation of a canon, for example, a set of texts is singled out from the vast library of the world and defined as embodying the aesthetic and moral ideals of a culture—"the best that has been thought and done," as Matthew Arnold puts it. This set of texts is then asserted to be superior to all other literary products of that culture, or of any other culture. In the construction of genre, literary works are categorized on the basis of form, and certain forms (epic and tragedy, for example) are asserted to be inherently superior, while others (autobiography and the novel, for example) are degraded. Finally, in the construction of the relation of writer to critic, a rigid distinction is drawn between the act of producing and the act of interpreting a literary work, and a battle ensues over which is the more essential enterprise. And because such battles for supremacy are premised on the validity of the categorical distinctions upon which they are based, the bellicose literary mind is always vexed by writing and writers who refuse to stay in their proper place.

This book is perhaps most unusual in its challenge not to a particular literary canon but rather to the pervasive and largely unexamined categorical distinction, which prevails in both the academic and the publishing worlds, between the critic and the writer. When I first contemplated this book, I was told by a number of my colleagues that I would never get it published because I was "mixing genres," and indeed that was precisely the response I received from the first publishing house to which I proposed the book. But, in fact, I am both a critic and a writer and, for me, the relation between the two activities is not hostile, but immensely fertile. The research and thinking I have done on how war is misrepresented in our fiction have inspired me to attempt fictional representations of my own which demilitarize our memories of war. Intersecting the essays and echoing their preoccupations, my stories seek to create memories of war less conducive, I hope, to waging war. These narratives displace the soldier as the mouthpiece of war, reminding the reader that the makers of war are not its only victims. The stories assume that women, children, noncombatants, and the enemy have an experience of war as much worth telling and remembering as is the story of any soldier. And the stories insist on the links between men and women at war, men and women in books, and men and women at work, play, home, and in bed. The insight gained from thinking about war in fiction lies, for me, in the medium's demand that cultural presumptions and propensities be enacted in the particulars of a human life. These stories demonstrate how the ideas explored speculatively in the essays on war literature permeate the air we breathe and inform the lives we lead.

## NOTES

1. Doris Lessing, *Prisons We Choose to Live Inside* (New York, 1987), 9–10.
2. *Valley Advocate* [Greenfield, Mass.], March 20, 1989.
3. Vera Brittain, *Testament of Youth* (New York, 1980), 291.
4. Sandra Gilbert, "Soldier's Heart: Literary Men, Literary Women, and The Great War," *Signs* 8, no. 3 (1983): 422–50.
5. Doris Lessing, A *Small Personal Voice* (New York, 1975), 57.
6. Virginia Woolf, *Three Guineas* (New York, 1938), 105.

# War Stories

I don't know when I first heard the hurricane story—
it was my favorite and I wore my mother out with asking for
it—but I know it was after the war and we were in Albany and
life, I thought, was unnecessarily severe. The war was over and
my father was home and we were living in a basement on
Swan Street while he did his residency. It puzzled me that our
dingy street had such a promising name until I figured out that
swans were once here and someone was going to return them
someday. We ate hot dogs and beans and macaroni and cheese
and my sister and I got whooping cough in the winter and my
mother and father weren't getting along. There had been a
woman in Brazil, I learned years later, and my mother was
wishing she had kept the good job in New York she got right
out of college instead of letting the war rush her into marriage
and kids.

Into my windowless bedroom below Swan Street, the hurricane story came like sunshine at midnight and I couldn't get
enough of it. I knew it by heart long before I knew it was a war
story. It was enough to content me for years, that a natural catastrophe should be remembered with such relish.

We're in the kitchen looking for rope in three feet of water.
We're an arm's length apart, Carol and me, and I can't hear a
word she's saying for the rain and the wind pounding on the
window. Through a river I see the garage collapse on the car.

The bow of a yacht cuts right between my eyes, veers off into the living room of the house next door. There's nothing out there but beach houses and heaving water. Some of the beach houses are heaving too, some are missing.

We're looking for rope to tie you two kids into the crib. Your Aunt Carol and I can't swim, of course, but we've got it all figured out. We've boarded up the sides of the crib and when this house collapses we're going to sail over to Uncle Austen's. We have the key and we can see his house is still standing.

So, we tie you two in and you don't like it a bit and howl worse than the wind so we have to untie you and take our chances.

We shouldn't be on the island obviously. Your father's mother turned red when she heard we were still out here. But we'd been alone on this strip of sand with you two babies for all of September, most of October, with nothing to do but play with you, listen to the radio, walk on the beach, and look out for tankers. We'd been half hoping for a German sub by the time we heard the hurricane was coming and we didn't want to miss it. Besides we didn't think it would be so bad, we got a lot of false alarms along the coast that fall—mines, subs, threats of invasion. We figured the hurricane wouldn't pan out either.

We admit we are wrong, but not before the causeway to the mainland is under water, so we drive back home, bundle you girls up in all your sleepers, and make popcorn. We make popcorn and we make a fire in the fireplace and we turn on the radio and we hear how its getting worse until we can't hear anything anymore for the rain and the wind and the roar of the surf. We huddle together on the sofa and I tell you the story about how, after my daddy died, my mama was afraid of thunder, so she'd wake up all four of us kids and herd us around the stove in the kitchen. She said she didn't want us to be afraid but we weren't, not even the littlest of us. We loved a good thunderstorm, wouldn't have wanted to miss it.

When I finish the story I notice the water oozing under the front door, so I put out the fire and Carol packs you two up and we each carry one of you upstairs. That's when we have the idea about the crib. I wade out to the garage for plywood, nails, and a hammer. Carol tells you two we're making a boat. By the time we think of the rope, there's three feet of water in the kitchen and the garage has collapsed on the car.

It gets worse before it gets better, but by now you girls are asleep and Carol and I are rocking absently by candlelight. There's no point trying to talk, we tried praying but it didn't work, so Carol knits and I think over the story I put you girls to sleep with. You were scared of floating away so I told you about how my mama found me floating on a pond and brought me back alive to her. Suddenly it's quiet and we know we are in the eye. We can hear the babies breathing, the candle doesn't flicker, we stop rocking. "It's going to be over," Carol whispers and its as though I've heard a leaf drop. And then I can't stop laughing.

Then she'd laugh the laugh I'd listen after for days, and wind up the story. "In the morning," she'd say, "the sun was shining and the coast guard brought you milk."

My sister, Catherine now, Katie when my mother told stories, was old enough to have recollections of her own of that hurricane. She told me one night, after Mother had laughed the laugh and wound up the story with the sunshine and the coast guard and the milk, that the coast guard had brought more than milk and sunshine. The coast guard had brought breakfast and lunch and dinner and drinks and toys and ice cream sundaes. They had dug out the car and rebuilt the garage and floated tinker toy convoys across the living room until the water went down. They wanted, Catherine recalled another night years later in her spacious Los Angeles living room with a laugh that was almost my mother's, to put the crib in the Shipbottom Coast Guard Museum.

When I saw the connection between the hurricane story and the invasion story, I was sweating under my coat in the hall of my elementary school during an air-raid drill. We had them often during the Korean War, and they scared me more than any hurricane ever did, even the one that blew the doors off the Catholic church the very moment my divorced uncle said, "I do." They kept us under our coats forever that day— two kids fainted and I realized all at once that we were a household of women during the hurricane because there was a war on across the ocean that threatened, any moment, to wash over to us. The invasion story was fresh in my mind, my mother had told it to me the night before as I lay, stiff and awake, trying to pinpoint enemy engines amidst the steady stream of passenger flights in and out of Newark Airport. "Poor duck," mother had said. "I don't know why you suffer so," and then she kissed my forehead and told me the story.

We're on the beach every morning, faithful as the seagulls and the fog, sifting sand for signs of the enemy. We've been issued binoculars, assigned the strip of beach between 20th and 30th streets, ordered to report every afternoon at five o'clock to the coast guard tower next to that dead end of a fishing boat they named the town after. You and Katie get splinters from the rotten wood and careen off the concrete pylons of the tower into the sand while Carol and I make our "report." The coast guard has issued you pins that say "I'm a Coast Guard Kid," and you wear them on your jackets by day, your pajamas by night. Katie thinks she's in the war now, elevated to active service, and she takes to the idea of duty. You take to whatever Katie takes to.

So there we are late one afternoon, ready to report the six tankers anybody can see hovering on the edge of the horizon. You and Katie, your pins flapping like medals over your hearts, are playing Pinocchio in the belly of the whale when the coast guard tower comes alive. Jeeps slide around the corner of 20th Street, screech to a halt at the beachhead. Uniforms scurry like ants up and down the zigzag ladder to the tiny cabin at the top of the tower. You and Katie must think this cabin is heaven, the way you beg and whine to go up there. Carol intercepts a man we know from the hurricane and asks what's going on. "German sub," he shouts over his shoulder. "Five miles out.

After the tankers. Maybe an invasion." And then he is gone in the jeep he blew in on, and the cabin is empty and we four are alone on the beach ready to report.

At sunset we sit on the bench at our beachhead like four ducks in a row, solemnly taking turns with the binoculars. Six tankers hang on the horizon like puppets before the show. As night creeps over us, we spot the coast guard trawlers, only they and the night are moving, then nothing happens until the moon is out and you girls have each found a separate star to wish on, and you are asleep and we are wishing we had blankets. Then we hear a rumbling, like the ocean is growling or turning over in its sleep, then flashes like fireflies pepper the horizon. A sudden burst lands on the six tankers and two trawlers like a spotlight. It is pitch dark again by the time we hear the explosion. It knocks Carol and Katie off the bench. I grab you with one hand, the bench slats with the other, and we ride the wave so smooth you never wake up. But Katie is awake, no story soothes her, not even the one about mama and the thunderstorms. She huddles under her jacket in the pantry all night, moaning that the Germans are coming.

The next morning we go down to the beach and it is covered with tar. The horizon is empty and we find a sticky boot that says L. L. Bean and a fishing lure like a tar baby. We deliver them faithfully to the coast guard tower, where we find out that a tanker sank and the German sub slipped away. The only invasion is the invasion of the tar: tar on the sheets, tar in your hair, tar under your fingernails, tar caked between your toes. You come back from the beach like ducks, fingers and toes webbed with tar, and I sit you down on the back steps and go at you with the turpentine. The tickling is unbearable and you hoot and howl and writhe and kick. I decide,

and here she laughed the laugh I recalled in the dark hot space under my coat during the air-raid drill, "I decide I'd rather have the Germans."

When they shouted "Better dead than red" at us at the Oakland factory where we were handing out leaflets for an anti-

Vietnam demonstration, I remembered how my mother felt about the Germans. And when I was learning how to shoot a rifle at the Piedmont Gun Club, I remembered how we had sat the night of the invasion, four ducks in a row. But only when Telegraph Avenue was lined with barbed wire and sharpshooters and the National Guard was camped in my backyard, did I realize I was in the invasion we had expected. And only when I actually saw that the barbed wire was razor wire and that the soldier on the roof of the Café Med was training his telescopic rifle on me and cocking the trigger and laughing, did I remember a story my mother told me only once, when I was sixteen and she and my father were getting divorced and I found her sitting on Dad's side of the bed with a gun on her lap. The drawer of his bedside table was pried open and I didn't think she knew I was in the room until she started talking. "They all came home from the war with guns, you know." She didn't touch the gun, just stared at it like it had dropped from the ceiling. "None of us liked it one bit. The best we could do was wrap them up and put them up high where you kids wouldn't get at them. But your Dad wanted his in his bedside table," her head dropped like a dead flower, "and the best I could do was make him get a lock on the drawer." She didn't move and I wanted to leave but she didn't let me.

During the war, they all have their guns on them, of course. Even the street cleaner has joined something or another that lets him carry a gun while he wets down streets where nobody lives but women and kids. It changes things, gives you a turn, knowing every man out there has a gun. Carol comes home from the market saying, "Guess who's got one now?" until there isn't a man left on the island to guess except the old German Jew who sells sea-shell lamps and has nothing to live for.

The coast guard thinks we should have a gun in the house. "The enemy is everywhere," they intone because it has been intoned to them, "even in our midst." "Just yesterday," Jimbo tells me a few days after the tar comes in, "we came across a guy hiding out in the Watson house. Saw a light on in the

garage. Took a couple pot shots at it and this guy runs out
whimpering he's a C.O. That means," Jimbo snorts, "See you
when the war's over."

Jimbo's story doesn't worry me, except the part about the pot
shots, and I don't think a gun will do us much good if the Germans come, but I don't like having nothing but my mouth to
put between us and all these men with guns. When I tell Carol
I think it's dumb being the only ones in the war without a gun,
she says flat out, "You bring a gun in this house and I'm leaving."

"She took the same line, you know, when your Uncle Tom
brought his home after the war." My mother looked up, inviting me to come closer now, to sit by her and the gun on Dad's
side of the bed. "Carol spent three cold weeks in November
alone at the shore waiting for him to give it up."

So we are gunless in a sea of guns the night Carol and I are
reading upstairs and hear noises in the garage. We pull back
the blackout curtains and see a flashlight beam glance across
the car. You girls are sleeping, even the ocean breathes softly,
and there's no moon. When the flashlight goes out, the darkness is so thick we know our two heads framed in the window
are sitting ducks.

I drop the curtain and hiss at Carol, "I expect whoever's out
there has a gun." Carol just shrugs and says, "I'll handle it.
You stay here with the girls," and down the stairs she goes in
her bathrobe. I think of letting her go alone, think it serves her
right, but I can't do it.

When I catch up with her, she is shining a flashlight around
the backyard and asking politely, "Is there anyone here?" I
knock the flashlight out of her hand trying to turn it off, "Why
don't you just say, 'Shoot me'?" I whisper too loudly as the
flashlight comes to rest a few feet from us, the beam probing
the garage entrance. Just then a figure crosses the beam and I
swear I would have shot it if I had a gun.

"I am sorry to frighten you." The voice is a woman's and

she speaks with some difficulty. "I live now across the street and I think I see a man in here. I am afraid for you and your girls."

"If I had had a gun," my mother touched the gun in her lap at last, "I would have killed her." She picked up the gun, stood and pointed it at my forehead, driving her lesson home. Then she stooped to kiss the place where the bullet would have gone in. "It's time I got rid of this," she said, walking to the door, "before someone gets hurt."

I never saw the gun again but the bucket of turpentine still stood by the back steps when my mother and I and my three-year-old daughter visited Carol at the shore a year ago. Since the birth of my daughter, I had grown obsessed with the threat of nuclear war. I couldn't bear the future I was offering her, and I hoped the shore and the household of women might give me courage to face it. After forty years the beach was nearly clean, and I dipped my feet in the bucket mostly for old time's sake, but my daughter wouldn't go near it. She cherished the two black spots on her feet like Catherine and I had our coast guard pins. She didn't remember when tar was the enemy, didn't know the meaning of invasion, didn't yet suspect anyone of wanting to blow her up. I put her down for her nap—just a hint of tar on the sheets—and joined Carol and my mother shelling peas on the front stoop.

"I always shell peas at the shore," Carol looked up at me and smiled, "in memory of my mother."

Even I remembered the stout German matron shelling peas on the front stoop. In the middle of August, she'd be there in corset, slip, dress, apron, stockings and shoes, shelling peas in the shade of a beach umbrella. She never set foot on the beach but no one passed her stoop without a word with her.

"In memory of the mothers," my own said softly, but she looked angry as she gazed up the street at the bench where we had sat out the invasion, and there on the front stoop time stood still and the war stories slipped into place, as a sailboat slipping across a sunset makes of an ocean a view.

# The War Zone:

## *The Great War and Modern Memory*

Canons and cannons have more in common than the accident of sounding alike. The very idea of a literary canon is tainted at the source with belligerence and a project of cultural imperialism. In her study of the response of the American academic community to World War I, Carol Gruber points out that in the fall of 1918 most American institutions of higher learning voluntarily "turned their intellectual and physical resources over to the War Department, and became centers for military training."[1] In other words, in 1918 America's liberal arts colleges and universities became schools for soldiers. Before the War Department took direct control of higher education, government officials had concluded that the war effort would require the cultural indoctrination of the male college population of the country, and the Committee on Education and Special Training had already issued a directive to the academic community to institute a War Issues course, "a course in the underlying and immediate causes of the war and in the conflicting points of view of the belligerent nations as expressed in their forms of government, their philosophies, and their literatures" (*MM* 238). The intention of the War Issues course was "to enhance the morale of the members of the corps by giving them an understanding of what the war is about and of the supreme importance to civilization of the cause for which we are fighting" (*MM* 239). In other words, the War Issues course would use the liberal arts to instill in American young men a conviction of their cultural superiority over the enemies of the state. Cruder versions of the course interspersed self-congratulation with pot shots at Germans (at the University of Michigan, for example, students were taught that "the English more than any other people in the world, except the French and ourselves . . . have the humanitarian spirit, a desire for fair play and to do what is right. . . . I think you would find that the Germans carry on war as they have in France and Belgium because the German people do not have the humanitarian spirit of fair play, which the English, American and French do have" [*MM* 240–41]). More sophisticated versions (such as the course at Columbia College which would provide the model, after the Great War was won, for the college's Western Civilization course, for years the jewel in the crown of its undergraduate program for men) canonized English and American culture. If our cause was to be our culture itself (our "supreme importance to civilization"), then our culture would need its saints and heroic exploits, manifest signs of its supreme importance. And, indeed, in a letter to the *New York Times*, Cyrus Veeser contends that the idea of canonization itself, as we use it in today's English and Comparative Literature departments, has its roots, at least in this country, in the War Issues course, called refreshingly baldly at the time of its inception, "thinking bayonets."[2]

Carol Gruber concludes *Mars and Minerva* with the observation that "the articulation of interest between the higher learning and the world of power that took place during the war's span was not an ephemeral experience" (259). The sixties and early seventies taught us again (or, at least, should have) to expect links between political power and cultural elites, and most oppressed groups in this country have come to recognize that acceptance of the artifacts of their members is a crucial step in the process by which they gain recognition as fully human producers of culture, not merely its beneficiaries. While the canon constructed from the War Issues course via Columbia College's Western Civilization course—a canon rooted in the unacknowledged assumption that the producers of artifacts of "supreme importance to civilization" are just about always white men—prevailed for nearly fifty years, it has been steadily eroded over the last two decades by challenges from highly accomplished members of excluded groups and cultures whose work has been recognized to be of considerable importance to civilization as well. So canons have proliferated since the sixties, and most subscribers to the canon constructed for the First World War have come to acknowledge the legitimacy of other bodies of literature and to admit into their own ranks a handful of representatives of once-excluded groups and cultures. Some form of a course on women writers, for example, is now offered at most American colleges and universities, and most courses in "great" literature include at least token women writers. In the last twenty years, a countercanon of women writers has been successfully implanted inside academe, and that canon, in turn, has already spawned a countercanon of women writers of color.

The steady pressure over the last two decades to expand our definition of who produces literature worth reading, and to break up the monopoly on culture worth preserving exercised by white Anglo-Saxon men, has been in some cases quite effective (e.g., women writers, African-American literature), but nowhere has it had *less* impact than on our literature of war. The literature that creates America's memory of its wars is, like the literature that girded American young men for World War I, almost exclusively the product of white English and American men. It is even possible to detect, in English and American literature on World War I, that canon in formation, to trace the process by which a various and diverse body of literature was constricted to the literature of a few which, in turn, became known as *the* literature on the Great War.

An idea of what constitutes that body of literature seems to have consolidated only after World War II reawakened interest in the literature of the war that preceded it, though individual collections of World War I poetry had begun to appear by 1915 and continued to appear with some frequency throughout the twenties and thirties. Frederick Brereton's influential *Anthology of War Poems* came out in 1930; Robert Nichols's *Anthology of War Poetry 1914–1918*, in 1943; and Edmund Blunden's *War Poets 1914–1918*, in 1958. The poets represented in these anthologies were those upon whom, in the sixties, two substantial critical studies of World War I literature would be based: John H. Johnston's *English Poetry of the First World War: A Study in the Evolution of Lyric and Narrative Form* (1964) and Bernard Bergonzi's *Heroes' Twilight: A Study of the Literature of the Great War* (1965). Though the memoirists of the war were slower to publish their work and to achieve recognition, by the mid-sixties a consensus had been reached on the names of the "classic" poets and memoirists of the Great War, and it was a consensus that was reached without any serious consideration whatsoever of the work of any woman writer.

Paul Fussell's *The Great War and Modern Memory* (1975) popularized in the United States what had already taken shape in England as a canon of World War I literature. Fussell's book was extraordinarily influential in establishing what American intellectuals still generally agree to be the central preoccupations, the sources, the form, and the terrain of war literature. Although a detailed study of the literature of only World War I, and of that literature "sharply narrowed,"[3] as Fussell acknowledges in his preface, *The Great War and Modern Memory* has largely determined what we in America call our literature not only of that war but also of all our wars since. So, to study Fussell's book and the scholarly traditions upon which it is based is, in part, to study the installation of a canon and to uncover the process by which a particular group of authors and texts comes to be known as *the* literature on a given subject, while others books on the same subject are forgotten. Most critics would have us believe that their own canon, at least, reflects merit, but Fussell's book and the books on which he grounds his work prove, however unwittingly, that preconceptions about the sex, class, race, nationality, and military record of the author operate before any weighing of the literary merit of the work. Fussell not only monumentalizes a very particular group of writers and books, he also shapes our recollection of war, creating for us a "modern memory" of twentieth-century warfare. And since, in contemporary America, few of us have our own wars to remember, Fussell's construction of war memories for us has considerable authority. Let us turn, then, to *The Great War and Modern Memory* with two distinct, but not unrelated, questions in mind: How does a canon get installed? and What is enshrined in this particular canon?

Let's begin with the book jacket. We see on the cover the name of the book in bold letters and the name of Paul Fussell in almost equally bold letters directly underneath, but also directly above a poignant picture of a World War I dog soldier. Leaning against the scarred trunk of a tree, the narrow-shouldered boy stares despondently at the ground. He carries no gun, bears no insignia or mark of rank. A sorry nameless bloke caught up in events too big for him, he's a tragic victim, not a culpable purveyor of war. Before we open the book, then, our attention is drawn to a particular war, to men as victims of that war, and to the presumption that war in fact is categorically different from war in retrospect, from war in literature.

The process of forging our memory of war begins on the cover of the book; the process of canonization begins on the inside of the book jacket, where the first thing we encounter is the voice of Lionel Trilling lionizing the book: "An original and brilliant piece of cultural history and one of the most deeply moving books I have read in a long time." Trilling draws on his authority as a widely known literary historian of the period to assure us we are getting reliable literary history here, but he also promises us a "deeply moving" experience, a promise rarely tendered in the world of literary criticism. Speculating on what might be so "deeply moving" in a genre that typically appeals to the intellect rather than the emotions, we return in imagination to the picture we have just encountered on the cover of the book, to that poor sorry bloke caught up in events too big for him.

The blurb that succeeds Trilling's celebration of Fussell's work presents Fussell's selection and interpretation of war literature as an already established historical given:

> Reflecting this change in attitudes, writers such as Sassoon, Graves, Owen, and David Jones created a new iconography and forced new images of violence into the language. Their writings considered here, together with contemporary newspaper and magazine accounts, and with private letters and diaries by ordinary but surpris-

ingly literate soldiers, became assimilated and imprinted in the collective consciousness of the twentieth century. Thus for later writers on other wars—especially such novelists as Mailer, Pynchon, and Vonnegut—the British Great War emerged as the original paradigm for much that seems murderous and absurd today.

This blurb informs us that a single "collective consciousness of the twentieth century" about war exists. It insinuates that this universal collective consciousness is rightly constructed by literate soldiers (and, in passing, that it is surprising for "ordinary" soldiers to be literate). And, finally, it instructs us that the paradigm for thinking about war is the *British* Great War and that the legitimate heirs of the "great tradition" of war literature are Mailer, Pynchon, and Vonnegut. A canon of World War II literature is taking shape here, right before our eyes.

Having studied the cover and read the blurb on the inside jacket, we will not be slow to grasp the implications of Fussell's dedication of his book:

To the Memory of
Technical Sergeant Edward Keith Hudson, ASN 36548772
Co. F, 410th Infantry
Killed beside me in France
March 15, 1945.

Now we understand Lionel Trilling's "deeply moving" a little better; this is not just a critical book, this is a memorial to a fallen comrade-in-arms. "Killed beside me in France," Fussell tells us, directing our attention not only to the dead soldier but also to the soldier fighting beside him. Thus Fussell quietly settles his own claim to the authority to write about the literature of war. He is a soldier; he, too, has been under fire, has seen a close friend die in combat, and he knows the code, he knows what all those military numbers, abbreviations, and designations mean.

Though we are still in the realm of pretext, we have already learned that British and American soldiers write our literature of war, that British and American soldiers write our literature on our literature of war, and that *The Great War and Modern Memory* has perhaps more in common with the Tomb of the

Unknown Soldier or the Vietnam Memorial in Washington than it has with what we normally call cultural history. Normally, we call cultural history in the elegiac mode sentimental fiction (e.g., *Gone with the Wind*).

In the preface that immediately follows the dedication, Fussell uses the word "myth" to describe the literature of war, but he stresses the power of myth as a determinant of human experience:

> I have tried to understand something of the simultaneous and reciprocal process by which life feeds materials to literature while literature returns the favor by conferring forms upon life. And I have been concerned with something more: the way the dynamics and iconography of the Great War have proved crucial political, rhetorical, and artistic determinants on subsequent life. At the same time the war was relying on inherited myth, it was generating new myth, and that myth is part of the fiber of our own lives. (GW ix)

Fussell presents the literary process of "conferring forms upon life" as an entirely genial, agentless, and benign one. "Literature" does it, and in so doing, it returns a favor. Though Fussell clearly acknowledges the power of literature to shape our thinking about war, he is markedly reticent about the intentions of the producers of that literature. Fussell also obscures his own part in the production of myths about war, presenting himself as an observer of rather than an agent in the process.

Though Fussell says he is "suggesting the forms of that myth," not forming it, he immediately proceeds to list the "writers who have most effectively memorialized the Great War as an historical experience with conspicuous imaginative and artistic meaning" (GW ix). Siegfried Sassoon, Robert Graves, and Edmund Blunden are the "classic memoirists"; "David Jones, Isaac Rosenberg, and of course Wilfred Owen" are "the poets of very high literary consciousness" (GW ix). Having singled out the "great" writers of World War I, Fussell adds, "And to see what the ordinary man has to say about it all, I have compared the scores of amateur memoirs lodged in the collections of the Imperial War Museum" (GW ix). Fussell, here, places beyond the realm of imagination the possibility that the ordinary or extraordinary woman might have something to say about it all, or that any noncombatant might have a word to add.

Fussell's next stroke is a breathtakingly exclusionary one, in spite of his vague hint that his rationale for drawing the line where he does may be incorrect.

> Correctly or not, the current idea of "the Great War" derives primarily from images of the trenches in France and Belgium. I have thus stayed there with the British Infantry, largely disregarding events in Mesopotamia, Turkey, Africa and Ireland, and largely ignoring air and naval warfare. By thus narrowing my view, I have hoped to sharpen it to probe into the origins of what some future "medievalist" may call The Matter of Flanders and Picardy. (GW ix–x)

Fussell reveals the extent to which his view of World War I is formed by British literary tradition rather than evoked by specific historical events when he rather wistfully hopes his book may be read in the very distant future as a companion to England's medieval war romances (those very romances, he will argue later in the book, that lured young English men to war). He betrays the unacknowledged assumptions that govern what literature is included in that tradition when he accepts, "correctly or not," "the current idea of 'the Great War'" (GW ix), an idea that seems to be just hanging around but that nonetheless licenses him to indulge one of the most deeply ingrained habits of the British imperial imagination, the habit of disregarding violence inflicted on the inhabitants of the Middle East, Africa, and Ireland.

Fussell concludes his preface with thanks to three institutions whose kindness eased his work on his book. The book was generously backed by Rutgers University, the National Endowment of the Humanities, and the Imperial War Museum and "its courteous staff." Fussell's ways of seeing war, we can deduce, are at least not repugnant to those of the state of New Jersey, the United States government, and the British war museum. Fussell also thanks several colleagues and critics, singling out a few for special attention. B. H. Liddell Hart is called the "prince of modern military critics," Richard Poirier's book on Norman

Mailer is labeled "authoritative." As Fussell's book presumes to identify the writers of interest on the Great War, so his preface identifies the critics deserving of our attention.

Contemporary reviewers of *The Great War and Modern Memory* accepted, without comment, the writers Fussell designated as the classic memoirists and poets of the war. None challenged Fussell's omission of all literature by women and civilians, none challenged his assumption that war literature is written by and about soldiers at the front. A considerable number of reviewers were deeply moved, just as Trilling said they would be, and more than one was struck by Fussell's dedication of the book to his fallen comrade-in-arms. In his extensive and useful survey of the literature on World War I in *Sewanee Review* in 1976, George Garrett reserved the word "definitive" for Fussell's book, and wrote of its memorial inscription, "that dedication, an epitaph and a memorial in form, haunts the whole book, casts a shadow like a single military cross." In the *Saturday Review*, W. H. Pritchard measured *The Great War and Modern Memory* in terms of its adequacy as a tribute to the fallen soldier: "I can't imagine a more humanly wise and compassionate tribute to him than this book provides." Most reviews were glowing, though F. A. Pottle, in *Yale Review*, accused Fussell of drawing too negative a picture of war, of leaving out its glories and its exaltations, while Pearl K. Bell of *The New Leader*, one of the two women reviewers I unearthed, challenged Fussell's willful blindness to modern technological warfare (to the navy and the air force) and questioned his tendency to identify World War II with World War I.[4] Though Fussell's composite portrait of men at war troubled various of his critics for various reasons, most would have subscribed, I believe, to Garrett's conclusion that the book is "as close to being 'definitive' as any single work can be, [and that] it is a superb example of the power of civilized criticism."

While Fussell urgently resists the glorification of war and the warrior which continues to be so marked a strain in most of our representations of war even today—and in this sense he does perform an act of "civilized criticism"—his interpretation of what constitutes war literature is stunningly narrow and has gone remarkably unchallenged. War literature is written by a handful of literate British and American soldiers, and it is selected, interpreted, and evaluated by the same. War literature, correctly or not, can afford to ignore war in the Middle East, Africa, and Ireland. It can afford to ignore war as it is experienced by women and civilians and the modern, high-tech army. A platoon of soldiers who fought on the Western front is licensed here to shape our culture's imagination of war.

The memory of World War I Fussell constructs for a generation of Americans stinging from Vietnam is the memory of innocence betrayed. "*Ex post facto,*" Fussell writes in his penultimate paragraph, "literary narrative has supplied [the Great War] with coherence and irony, educing the pattern: innocence savaged and destroyed" (GW 335). "Educing the pattern" is deftly put; it is impossible to determine where this pattern originates: in the war? in the literature of the war? in the mind of Paul Fussell? Whether the pattern reflects the actual experience of soldiers in World War I, or the way they and/or Paul Fussell like to remember those days, it points to a structure of feeling of remarkable persistence and resilience in our literature of war. After war after war after war, that innocence is re-created which the next war will destroy. "It is war," Neil McCallum tragically discovers on the battlefields of World War II, "and to believe it is anything but a lot of people killing each other is to pretend it is something else, and to misread man's instinct for murder."[5] Yet, Paul Berlin, in Tim O'Brien's novel, *Going after Cacciato*, goes to Vietnam no less innocent for having the betrayals of two world wars behind him, and Philip Larkin, in the early sixties, can still imagine the soldiers of World War I as "sweet generous people who pressed forward and all but solicited their own destruction" (GW 19). The idea fighting for survival here, it seems to me, is the idea that men go to war not *really* knowing that killing other people is what war is all about. And the story that keeps this idea alive and close to our hearts is the story of the soldier's tragic discovery on the battlefield that what he is a part of is killing.

In the canon of war literature to which Fussell subscribes, the cultural elite of the men who fight our wars (i.e., white British or

American soldiers well-versed in the canon of English literature)
pleads its case, in part by reconstructing the innocence the men
claim lured them into war in the first place. Ironically, the chief
instiller of the sweet innocence that drives men to war seems to
be literature. Fussell makes a strong case that the imagination of
the literate British soldier of World War I was crammed full of the
pseudo-medieval romances of Tennyson and William Morris,
and that these, like most of the classics of an English boy's
education of the period, offered a most appealing, a most alluring
view of the battlefield. "No nation," Barbara Tuchman points
out in her study of British accounts of their military exploits in
Burma in World War II, "has ever produced a military history of
such verbal nobility as the British" (quoted in GW 175). All the
memoirists of World War I upon whom Fussell dwells cast some
measure of blame on the great tradition of English literature for
sending them to war.

Fussell demonstrates that the canon of English literature and
the canonical education it produced, by celebrating warriors and
glorifying war, played a crucial role in readying young English
men to kill and die in World War I, but he seems to want to assert
that literature has since played a different part. Unlike the Vic-
torian romancers of war, the memoirists of World War I, Fussell
argues, wrote war as it really was, which should, in all logic, have
been the end of war, but it wasn't. Fussell struggles with this
contradiction in his more recent book on World War II, *Wartime: Understanding and Behavior in the Second World War*
(1989). "Those who fought the Second World War," he claims,

> didn't at all feel that it was good for them. For one thing, they had
> access to a lot of profoundly unbellicose literature not available to
> Brooke and his enthusiastic followers. If the troops of the Second
> War had not read, they'd at least heard of the general point made by
> Remarque's *All Quiet on the Western Front* and Barbusse's *Under
> Fire*, as well as by the sardonic memoirs of Robert Graves and
> Siegfried Sassoon. Many were familiar with Hemingway's under-
> standing of military experience as vividly unfair and dishonorable in
> *A Farewell to Arms*, as well as with Frederic Manning's exposure of

army life as not just pointlessly hazardous but bureaucratic, boring and chickenshitty in *Her Privates We*.[6]

Yet, in spite of this legacy of a "profoundly unbellicose literature," English and American men went to World War II in unprecedented numbers and with unprecedented enthusiasm. Either literature has no power, or the literature of World War I is not as "profoundly unbellicose" as it might appear. Though the literature of that war evoked grim truths about warfare with great verbal nobility, it continued to consecrate the fighting man and to extol his singular devotion to the men fighting beside him. Even in this literature of protest, war remains the manliest of occupations and manliness is understood not as an instinct to kill but as "grace under fire."

In his discussion of the tension between the nastiness of World War I and a "public language used for over a century to celebrate the idea of progress," Fussell observes: "The difficulty was in admitting that the war had been made by men and was being continued *ad infinitum* by them" (GW 169–70). Now, this strikes me as precisely the difficulty both Paul Fussell's book and the literature it enshrines do their best to evade. No one *makes* World War I, not in Fussell's book, not in the literature it celebrates. Fussell is deeply drawn to a trope he discovers in Edmund Blunden's *Mind's Eye*, a trope that makes war a player in the game, not the game men play. Of the infamous Battle of the Somme, Blunden writes, "Neither race had won, nor could win, the War. The War had won, and would go on winning" (quoted in GW 38). This fiction of the independent agency of war (the fiction that wars make themselves) lifts the burden of guilt from the men who declare and organize war, as well as from those who actually carry the guns and drive the tanks and drop the bombs. Politicians and soldiers may look like they are making war, but really they are not. Really they are victims, pawns of a force beyond their control, poor sorry blokes caught up in events too big for them.

The idea of the soldier as the chief victim of war permeates

Fussell's text and the memory it shapes of war. As George Garrett says, though in a different tone, the shadow of the military cross haunts the book. Fussell's first chapter, "A Satire of Circumstance," suggests that Thomas Hardy's collection of poems published under that title in November 1914 provides "a medium for perceiving the events of the war just beginning. It does so by establishing a terrible irony as the appropriate interpretative means" (GW 3). Hardy, with his oddly comforting faith in happenstance, his consoling view that men are not masters of their fate, offers the soldier a narrative that relieves him of all intention of being where he is or of doing what he's doing. As the iceberg just happens to be between the *Titanic* and its destination, so war lies in wait for men who have every reason to believe they are going somewhere else. The "appropriate interpretive means" Hardy provides constructs the soldier as the instrument of war, and war as a twist of fate, a catastrophe, an accident, maybe even an agent with an agenda of its own. And the appropriate interpretive tone, the ironic note Fussell discovers in text after text on World War I, and indeed in the war itself, similarly constructs the soldier as the passive victim of war. Fussell takes his definition of irony from Northrop Frye: "the mode in which the hero's power of action is less than ours is the 'ironic,' where 'we have the sense of looking down on a scene of bondage, frustration, or absurdity'" (GW 311). The ironic stance insists on the impotence of the hero; men "who once were like us in power of action . . . now have less power of action than we do" (GW 312). So the soldier, the wager of war, in the memory or myth Fussell constructs of him, comes to have less power of action in the arena of war than you or I do.

A story of war so tailored to obscure the causes of war and to assuage the consciences of the men who declare and fight wars would not survive as the dominant account our literature offers of war if it were not the only account of war we recognize. Without, I believe, a single conscious thought on the matter, Fussell and the critics and anthologists he draws on stake out a territory for war literature that excludes every account but that of the literate, British or American soldier. The locale of war literature is the front, the battlefield. The author of war literature has to have been there. If we accept this definition, there is little we can do but choose among the stories of soldiers.

What's so shocking when one casts an eye over the landscape of Fussell's book—and the book does have the character of a landscape, in part because Fussell's evocation of the Western front, of the mud and the trenches and the wire and the stench and the waste, is so graphic—is the utter absence of women. Women are nowhere to be seen. They are not at the front, they are not in the rear, they are not tending the home fires, they are not writing their memoirs. In the memory of the Great War Fussell constructs, the only memorable woman is A Little Mother, the enthusiast recalled in Robert Graves's *Goodbye to All That* who writes a letter to the editor of the *Morning Post* celebrating the sacrifice of British mothers who have given their sons to the war and passionately urging against the acceptance of any peace short of total victory. Since this requires, on Fussell's part, the deliberate suppression of women and texts he knows—he does mention in passing, for example, Vera Brittain's *Testament of Youth* and *Honourable Estate* and Virginia Woolf's *Jacob's Room*—he must have a reason for intensifying the androcentricity of what was already an intensely androcentric world. The myth Fussell means to instill of World War I, the memory he wants to create of soldiers as the tragic victims of war, can survive only if we imagine war as impinging on no one but soldiers. A popular fantasy for containing war designates an out-of-the-way chunk of the globe as a war zone. If you want war, you go there and get it; if not, you can walk around it. And it is to this fantasy that Fussell, I think, ultimately appeals. If we ignore the devastation wreaked by war on women, children, civilians, animals, the land, buildings, bridges, communications, the entire fabric of family, social and civilized life, we can perhaps construe the makers of war to be its victims, but this requires that we imagine the world of war to be inhabited only by soldiers, a setting for war willfully anachronistic in these days of atomic and guerrilla warfare and eerily reminiscent of the motel room Patrick Purdy left behind when he set out for the Stockton, California, schoolyard where he would spray the playing children with bullets from his assault rifle, killing five and ultimately himself. His room at the motel was empty but for a company of toy soldiers, a hundred at least, lurking in the closet, crouched in the drawers, hiding in the drapes, lying in ambush in the freezer.

*The Great War and Modern Memory* is more than fourteen years old now, and there'd be no reason to exhume it if it didn't still reign as the paradigm in this country for thinking literarily about war. With the noteworthy exception of H. Bruce Franklin's *War Stars: The Superweapon and the American Imagination* (1988), which traces the links between America's fictions of future wars and invincible weapons and our readiness to develop and use such weapons, most studies of the literature of war that have appeared since Fussell's have either added to his canon a list of like-minded authors and texts from World War II and Vietnam or challenged his selection of soldier's stories, but few have questioned his fundamental premises and strategies for recollecting war. Though Andrew Rutherford complains, in *The Literature of War: Five Studies in Heroic Virtue* (1978), of the anti-heroic bias of contemporary critics of war literature and offers a more militant collection of narratives and poems by British soldiers (a canon fathered by Kipling instead of Hardy), and Jeffry Walsh, in *American War Literature 1914–Vietnam* (1982), constructs a more distinctively American canon of war literature, both share Fussell's assumption that war literature is about men at the front.

Feminist response to war literature is still in its nascent stages. In an article called "Soldier's Heart: Literary Men, Literary Women, and the Great War"[7] which first appeared in 1983, Sandra Gilbert recognizes and demonstrates that a significant body of literature by women about World War I exists and that it tells a story rather different from the sad tale of the soldier. A more recent collection of feminist readings of the literature of war, *Arms and the Woman* (1989),[8] includes essays on women's memoirs and novels of World War I (Helen Zenna Smith's *Not So Quiet . . .* , May Sinclair's *Tree of Heaven*, and Willa Cather's *One of Ours*), but even these feminist challenges to the male canon focus on the memoir and the front. Though they expand the zone of war to include the "home front," they still imagine war as a particular place one is at in a particular historical moment.

The problem with Fussell's canon is not just that it gives white British and American soldiers an exclusive on suffering in war, though this is a crucial and startlingly obvious problem to go unremarked for so many years. But the memory of war Fussell constructs also discourages the formulation of certain kinds of questions about war and its relation to literature. Fussell's emphasis on the memoir, for example, inhibits thinking about war as a continuous and ongoing condition of twentieth-century life. The memoir consolingly frames war, limiting it to a particular place and time and insisting that, outside this particular place and time, there is no war to remember. The memoir thus sustains the increasingly untenable distinction between the war zone and the home front and between the soldier and the civilian, while it depicts war as an aberration rather than the habit of a culture. Doris Lessing, in *Shikasta*, takes a fundamentally different view of war when she refers to World War I and World War II as the First and Second Intensive Phases of the Twentieth-Century War. And because Fussell is invested in the process of canonization, because he both benefits and confers benefits as a result of his conviction that he knows which writers and critics are of supreme importance to civilization and which are not, he cannot raise questions about the bellicosity of this assumption of superiority or about the extent to which it is cultivated in the literature he values.

*No Man's Land*, the title of Sandra Gilbert and Susan Gubar's unfolding, monumental, multivolumed account of "the place" of the woman writer in the twentieth century, would seem to locate the First World War at the very center of the authors' analysis of the situation of the woman writer in our time. But war, in Gilbert and Gubar's construction, is not a historical event but a metaphor for the relation between the sexes. The real war of this century, in their view, is the war between the sexes fought out with words on the terrain of literature. Gilbert and Gubar flagrantly and relentlessly use the language of warfare, particularly the charged and heavily laden poetics of the Western front, to describe relations between women and men. *The War of the Words*, their first volume is subtitled, and the last will be *Letters from the Front*. In their preface, Gilbert and Gubar define no man's land as a "disputed domain" where "scattered armies of men and women all too often clash by day and by night," and they describe what they are offering in their literary history as an "account of sexual battle."⁹ The first chapter opens with two questions: "Is a pen a metaphorical pistol? Are words weapons with which the sexes have fought over territory and authority?" (*MNL* 3). Gilbert and Gubar's deployment of the military language Fussell helped make so richly metaphorical has its fine ironies, and *No Man's Land* graphically and amply documents that English and American men in this century did not express their bellicosity only at the front, nor did they leave it there or shed it with their uniforms. They brought it home and directed it at their mothers, wives, sisters, and women colleagues, and if they were men of letters, they directed it at women of letters. Gilbert and Gubar locate bellicosity at the very core of English and American patriarchal culture and they demonstrate how our canonical literature has fostered, disseminated, and rewarded the combative stance.

But when one casts an eye over the landscape of *No Man's Land*, one has certain shocks too. In a kind of topsy-turvy version of Fussell's narrative of war, the only people really suffering in Gilbert and Gubar's war story are women of letters. The metaphorical war between the sexes is so foregrounded, one loses sight of the real wars, of the massive, global human slaughter actually going on in the world outside these duels of the pen. And perhaps because Gilbert and Gubar have begun themselves to take the metaphor for the act, or perhaps because they see the war of the words as a war that women, or at least a few women, are winning at last, they exude a disconcerting enthusiasm for the bellicosity at the core of patriarchal English and American culture. *No Man's Land*, as the title forewarns, offers a literary landscape bristling with hostility and murderous intentions, a world where pens are not penises but guns, and words kill, where even our books are shooting at us, and the very best of them are marked by their enthusiasm for combat: "it is precisely his or her belligerent passion that generates texts marked by compelling intensity—often, indeed, by aesthetic excellence" (NML xiii). We like to think of literature and literary studies as an antidote to the bellicosity whose supreme expression is war and the wanton devastation of the human race, and I, for one, like to think of feminist literary criticism as an antidote to the bellicosity of patriarchal literature and literary studies. As a product of the imagination, literature has the potential to disrupt and transform the belligerent passions that permeate our culture. But literature also has its feet in the mud, and all too often our books, or our responses to them, encourage us instead to think bayonets.

The history of our reading of H. G. Wells's War of the Worlds offers a striking illustration of how our cultural presumptions can overwhelm an author's intentions. Written to expose the bellicosity of our culture, the novel has been misconstrued to promote it. Wells dedicated The War of the Worlds "To my brother, Frank Wells, This rendering of his idea."[10] In a 1920 edition of Strand Magazine, Wells explained this somewhat elusive dedication:

> The book was begotten by a remark of my brother Frank. We were walking together through some particularly peaceful Surrey scenery. "Suppose some beings from another planet were to drop out of the sky suddenly," said he, "and begin laying about them here." Perhaps we had been talking of the discovery of Tasmania by the Europeans—a very frightful disaster for the native Tasmanians! But that was the point of departure. (WW 119)

Wells's account of the origins of his narrative makes clear his intention that the British and other colonizing nations should recognize themselves in the Martians and that his text is meant to be a critique of their heartless slaughter of so-called primitive peoples in the name of the colonial enterprise. Yet, as H. Bruce Franklin points out in War Stars, the first response of the American literary imagination to The War of the Worlds (1897) was Garrett P. Serviss's sword-rattling Edison's Conquest of Mars (1898), in which the ingenious American inventor single-handedly exterminates the Martian race with his arsenal of high-tech weapons.[11] Serviss's response not only ignores Wells's critique of our bellicosity; it also reverses our place in the narrative. In his, and in all subsequent restagings of *The War of the Worlds*, Americans and British alike uniformly identify themselves not with the British but with the Tasmanians, not with the Martian invaders but with the tragic victims of a monstrous and inexplicable aggression.

## NOTES

1. Carol S. Gruber, *Mars and Minerva: World War I and the Uses of the Higher Learning in America* (Baton Rouge, 1975), 213. Hereafter referred to as *MM*.
2. Cyrus Veeser, "Western Culture Course Began in Indoctrination," Letters to the Editor, *New York Times*, June 23, 1988.
3. Paul Fussell, *The Great War and Modern Memory* (New York, 1975), ix. Hereafter referred to as *GW*.
4. George Garrett, "The Literature of the Great War," *Sewanee Review* 84 (1976); W. H. Pritchard, "High Diction in the Trenches," *Saturday Review*, Feb. 21, 1976; F. A. Pottle, "The First World War," *Yale Review* 65 (Summer 1976); Pearl K. Bell, *The New Leader* 58 (1975).
5. Neil McCallum, *Journey with a Pistol* (London, 1959), 107.
6. Paul Fussell, *Wartime: Understanding and Behavior in the Second World War* (New York, 1989), 130.
7. Sandra Gilbert's "Soldier's Heart: Literary Men, Literary Women, and the Great War" first appeared in *Signs* in 1983 and has reappeared since in Margaret Randolph Higonnet's *Behind the Lines: Gender and the Two World Wars* (1987), and, most recently, in *Sexchanges* (1989), the second volume of Gilbert and Gubar's *No Man's Land*.
8. Helen M. Cooper, Adrienne Auslander Munich, Susan Merrill Squier, eds., *Arms and the Woman* (Chapel Hill, 1987).
9. Sandra M. Gilbert and Susan Gubar, *No Man's Land: The Place of the Woman Writer in the Twentieth Century*, vol. 1: *The War of the Words* (New Haven, 1988), xiii. Hereafter referred to as *NML*.

10. H. G. Wells, *The Time Machine, The War of the Worlds*, ed. Frank D. McConnell (New York, 1977), 119. Hereafter referred to as *WW*.
11. H. Bruce Franklin, *War Stars: The Superweapon and the American Imagination* (New York, 1988), 66–68.

## The Time of Her Life

We are having Sunday afternoon dinner at Aunt Louise and Uncle Dick's house on State Street in Albany. We are living in a slum around the corner because Dad just got back from the war and he isn't a full-fledged doctor yet, but I eat once a week like a princess in the dining room with the fireplace with the tiles from Bavaria. It's years before the nightmares and Uncle Dick is still adorable, and I am laughing wildly at his imitation of a bear deciding if I am good enough to eat, when I notice Aunt Louise in the doorway playing charades. My mother sees her too, and when we both figure out that what Louise wants is me, I dive under the table but my mother catches me and hisses that there's no such thing as a free lunch, so up the stairs I go with Louise and up the stairs again and yet again, until we are on the very top floor in front of a door that's always locked. The key Louise takes out of her pocket looks like the kind they use to lock up crazy people and when the door opens, I expect something unspeakable to whoosh out in our faces, but all that happens is Louise shoves me in and the next thing I know the key is turning in the lock.

Skeletons in the sewing room, I hear Louise hiss before her heels click down the stairs and fade out and I realize I am locked up in a dark room that isn't empty. The first thing I see after I stop hollering since nobody can hear me is a woman bent over a sewing machine in front of a heavily curtained window. Or is it a sewing machine? Maybe it's a baby. And does it have to be a woman? Can't it be a soldier bending over his gun? I take a deep breath and rip back the curtain and in the harsh sunlight of mid-afternoon, I see a flag draped over a high-backed chair, the stripes bloodied and torn, the stars pocked with bullet holes. And what might have been a baby or a gun turns out to be a tiny replica of a battlefield where toy soldiers with spiked hats face toy soldiers with round hats, and wave upon wave of them fight and fall, fight and fall.

My mother always said Louise proposed to Uncle Dick. She might have told herself she was going to Hoboken to say good-bye to her brother, but since her brother and Dick were leaving for the Great War on the same boat, there was no way she could kiss one off and not the other. And besides, my mother would triumphantly add, only in Dick's ear did Louise whisper that she'd be waiting for him when he got back.

Certainly she would have gone to Hoboken to see her brother Austen off to the war. Only three remained of the family of six who had come to Albany from Bavaria at the turn of the century. And Edna, Louise's little sister, was already married and about to have a family of her own, so Austen must have been everybody to Louise, who could have no real life of her own until she married. There were her pupils, of course, but not many girls were learning German these days, and without Austen to cook for and his friends around the place, the town house on State Street must have seemed huge and empty, full of rooms belonging to the dead and gone. Certainly, she'd have gone the hundred miles to see Austen off at the dock, if only to postpone the moment when she turned the key in the heavy oak door of the home that was all hers now and stepped into the foyer to see the curving staircase with its long smooth banister arcing up into darkness and silence.

Dick was a gentleman, my mother used to say, the decentest, handsomest man she'd ever known. So when Louise said she'd wait, he took it to mean if he came back whole and she was on the dock, he'd have to marry her. And so it happened. Dick sailed back six months later without a scratch, Louise was there on the dock dressed in lavender and a picture hat, waving a matching lavender handkerchief and yodeling yoohoo, and they were married before the armistice was signed.

But who's to say Dick hadn't had his eye on her all along? She wasn't that much older than he was, two years at the most, and he'd been eating at her table for nearly a year before he went to war, so her proposal, if she made it, could not have been altogether out of the blue. And how dearly he loved her house— he lived in it until he died at ninety-one, and even when he'd forgotten Louise's name and had nothing in the kitchen to eat but a jar of peanut butter and a can of Spam, he could tell you the name of the Bavarian village represented in each of the sixteen tiles around the fireplace in the dining room.

And she'd have been good-looking enough. The oldest photo I know shows her standing with my father in front of Uncle Austen's house at the Jersey shore. My father is crisp and snappy in his World War II naval officer's uniform, and he stands with his arm around Louise, smiling broadly at whoever's taking the picture. Dick, likely as not. He was the one to bring the camera or the badminton set or the hula hoop. Louise has on the plain padded jacket, skirt to the knees, thick stockings, and sensible shoes women wore instead of uniforms during the war years, and her hair is rolled up on the sides and curled in front. She would be well into her forties by now, but her figure is slim and her face has good lines. Her eyes, though, are already quite hollow.

In my mother's story, however, Dick is the tragic victim, undone by doing right. And who's to say it isn't so? I never knew Louise before she was a casualty, and Dick's lips were sealed on the subject of his wife. I suppose my father knows a thing or two, but it's too late to ask.

They tell us kids that Louise is senile, but we don't believe it. They tell us our grandfather is senile too, and he is as batty as a loon. But he always reads us the comics in the newspaper as soon as it comes, and sometimes he wanders and we all get to go after him. I find him one day in the five and dime, reading a comic book out loud to a bunch of kids who aren't there, but he smiles like an angel when he sees me and reads the rest to me. We never get to go after Louise, but sometimes she's fun and plays mama bear to our Goldilocks and baby bear, but when we are laughing out loud and least expecting it, she turns and snarls like a real mama bear who hates us, and we scream and slink away and talk about who we should tell. We never tell anybody but we don't like being with Louise even when she's fun because we never can tell when she'll remember how she hates us.

Dick, on the other hand, we adore. Dick's birthday is on the fourth of July and he always wears shocking-pink bathing trunks. Every year he gets a new pair, and the next year he wears the pair he got the year before. And Dick chases us and snarls and snatches us and throws us sky-high, but it's always in fun. He never means it the way Louise does.

My mother's story is that what happened to Louise was that she couldn't have children. Dick loved children, my mother would point out, he'd have been the best of fathers. Remember how you kids used to pester him to death from the moment he arrived at the shore till the moment he left? Play bear, you'd demand, pawing his arms and nipping at his knees. Take us for blueberry ice cream in your Cadillac with the top down. Put on your pink bathing suit and take us to the beach. And he did, with a grin and a whistle, and he loved every minute of it. But poor Louise was barren—how we kids would dwell on that word. It means she's a desert, we'd whisper, a tree without a leaf; like a dried-up prune, we'd howl, like Antarctica. But Dick stuck to her, Dick stuck to her (my mother would always say this twice), though it cost him his heart's delight. We kids knew what that meant, we'd seen her snarl at him just like she snarled at us, but he stuck to her no matter what, though he peeled around in that powder-blue Cadillac convertible of his looking like he was having the time of his life, while she faded into the woodwork. There are dozens of pictures of Dick in his

shocking-pink bathing trunks, posing and grinning and drag-
ging somebody into the frame, though the color of the trunks
doesn't show until the late fifties when the album ends and his
thick black hair has already turned silver white. Shots of
Louise toward the back of the album fail to record a single
memorable feature. An instant after her image is seen, nothing
remains in the mind but the vague outline of a woman, or is it
a woman after all? A figure in a dense fog.

I've cut my foot on a shell on the beach. I must be nine or ten,
because I'm alone on the beach, and when I limp back to the
house, leaving a bloody track on the sidewalk and up the front
stairs, there's no one there but Louise. She's knitting a baby's
bootie on the front porch and I think she's going to pretend I'm
not here when suddenly the fog lifts from her eyes and they
smile like sunshine. She drops the bootie to hug me tight until
I stop crying and she doesn't even seem to mind that I'm
bleeding on her yarn. Propping me with pillows like a doll who
can't sit up right, she runs to the bathroom for the first aid kit.
While she ever so tenderly picks the grains of sand out of my
cut and paints it pink with Mercurochrome, she lets me
choose a band aid, any one I want, and sniff all the bottles that
have a skull and cross bones on the label. There, she says,
looking up at me with a smile so sweet I want to kiss her forehead and bury my nose in the musky scent of her hair, I've
done it. You won't even be limping by the fourth of July. And
then, as though her last words have shocked her lips, they
purse and utter a startled cry and the curtain comes down over
her eyes. She doesn't see me anymore, but she sees the blood
on the yarn and she mumbles over and over again, Skeletons
in the sewing room. Blood on the thread.

Others said (said to me? or did I overhear it? The story, like the
bathing trunks, seems too pink for my father's people. Hard-
working Germans, the women were bossy and thrifty, the men
worried about their money and their bowels. So maybe I made
the story up, or maybe it's what the women said to each other

when they thought no one was listening), others said Dick
never loved Louise and he should not have married her. In this
version, Dick marries Louise for her house and he carries on
for years with his strawberry-blonde receptionist, flaunting her
all over Albany in his powder-blue Cadillac convertible, making up, he says, for what Louise won't give him. In this story,
there's even a hint that it's Dick who can't have children, that
it's something he picked up in the war and he made up the
story about Louise being barren to put us off the track.

A skeleton is chasing me and he is carrying a big gun with a
knife on the end and he wears shocking-pink bathing trunks.
Sometimes he catches me and throws me sky-high and then I
am drifting down like a snowflake, or maybe I plummet like a
dead duck, but always I am going to land on the point of the
knife on the barrel of that gun and always I wake up before I
do.
    I still had a band aid on my foot but I wasn't limping on the
fourth of July when I first had this nightmare which pursued
me for months. I had never known a dream could recur so re-
morselessly. It came only once each night, so after I'd had it I
could get some rest, but until it came, I'd lie in a pool of sweat
with my eyes wide open chanting the names of the states and
capitals to keep awake. And I'd swear I am awake when that
skeleton slides through the door and I jump out the window
and land in the lilac bushes and think I am looking at the
azalea in full bloom when what I am really seeing is the shocking pink of the bathing trunks which hang like loose skin on
the pelvis of that thing which has already spotted me among
the lilacs, so I run and run until I'd plunge headlong into the
chest of my father, who'd shake his head and say, Another
nightmare?
    No dream had ever stalked me like that. It scared me to
death and because it was in my head, nobody could help me. I
told my mother, finally, what happened in the dream, but she
said that was a terrible way to think of Uncle Dick who loved
children and wouldn't hurt a flea and stuck to his wife even

though she was barren. So I tried to keep awake counting the good things about Uncle Dick, like when he took us to Barnegat Light in the convertible with the top down and we saw the sea gulls drowning in oil, or when he took us to see the fishing boat come in and we saw zillions of slimy fish flapping and flopping and gasping in the hold, but every recollection led to that skeleton sliding through the door, except the one that left me standing eyes wide open and breathless at the window of his room in Uncle Austen's house at the shore.

It's the fourth of July and it's going to be a scorcher and I want to be the very first this year to see Uncle Dick in his bathing trunks so I have put on my moccasins which make me quiet as an Indian and nobody knows I am at the window or even near the house. And I am the very first, not counting Uncle Dick, to see the shocking-pink trunks except they are falling down because he is so very lean, and I giggle as he bends to pull an old leather case from under the bed because I can see his crack. But I stop giggling when he opens the case and pulls out a funny metal hat with a spike on top and an ancient, evil-looking gun. I shudder when he attaches a big knife to the end of the barrel, but I would explode with laughter when he puts on the hat except he looks right at me and his eyes are ice. I am going to run away but my feet are glued to the ground and my legs don't work anymore so I have to watch him cradle the gun in his arms and plant a fond kiss on the sharp blade of the knife, like it's a baby's forehead. The hairline cut on his upper lip is already oozing a few drops of blood before I can tear my feet loose and I don't stop running until I am ten blocks down the beach under the hull of a ship wrecked in a hurricane during World War I.

Not long after the Cuban missile crisis, I got a letter from Dick. Birthday cards and Christmas cards with a ten-dollar bill inside and signed "The Big Bear" I'd come to expect, but he'd never written a letter. I thought maybe it had something to do with his will. He has no children of his own, my mother never

failed to remind me when I balked at writing the thank-you
notes or said I'd rather spend Easter with a friend. That we had
stood on the brink of a war which might have annihilated us
all had only briefly disrupted my really pressing concern with
what college sorority I should join, so years went by before it
occurred to me to connect Dick's letter with that flirtation with
World War III. Eight hand-written pages in an ink so thin it
was almost water, the letter opened with an eulogy to the glories of France—the beauties of its countryside, the delicate
bouquet of its wines, the generosity of its dark-eyed women.
And when the letter came to the trenches, the ecstatic grew
somber to call up the mud and the blood and the awestruck
eyes of the mouldering dead, and then the somber turned
tragic to give tribute to the dear comrade who laid down his
life for his friend, and whose ghost preserved that friend once
again when his body lay rigid with fear in the wastes of no
man's land, whose ghost returned to swaddle his friend in the
flag of his country and sing him deeply deeply to sleep. And
the Golden Virgin of the Basilica of Albert, clutching the baby
Jesus in her outstretched arms, had leaned over Dick with tears
in her supplicating eyes, and Dick had stood in Maple Copse
near Sanctuary Wood on the very spot where the crucified Ca-
nadians had taken so very long to die, and he had seen with his
own eyes the Wild Men, that savage company of deserters
from both sides who lived like moles under no man's land and
crawled out from their secret lairs on moonless nights to plun-
der the dead and the living dead. And Dick had been drunk on
air, and he had heard the nightingale sing to the beat of the
German 88s, and he had looked up one morning from the
trenches at a hawk riding the wind and he had known for a
moment, but to know for a moment was to know for all time,
that air had substance and was of him and would be him
should he be called to lay down his sorry carcass in the mud,
and Dick had had the time of his life.

I am looking for Louise's head. If I can find it in time I can put
it back on. I have come to a house, all corridors and staircases

and shut doors. In the hallway I find myself in, red and white doors alternate with patches of blue wall. Whispers swell, crash, and retreat behind closed doors like the ocean I heard as a child from the bed under the eaves at my grandmother's house at the shore. I open a door and I fall, am falling, no, sliding now, yes sliding down the great winding banister of Dick and Louise's four-story town house, a bobsled run of a banister ride and, as I plummet toward the great coil at the bottom, the twist and flip of the newel post which, if you don't jump off in time, wraps you, wham, right round the knobby knees of the hat rack, as I glide I see, only for an instant but an instant is long enough to see Louise's head, not even hanging properly on a hook, but tossed carelessly, like a muddy soccer ball or a torn rubber boot, between the three lion's paw feet of the hat rack.

Louise died a few weeks after Saigon fell, and I went to her funeral because I was on the road, putting behind me what I had seen on TV the night Saigon fell. Dick mistook me for a woman he'd known in the signal corps in World War I. He clasped my hand in both of his, as though I were the one in mourning, and said he'd heard how my fiancé had been shot down in Bavaria. A woman, he said, stroking my hand, never lives that down.

In her casket, Louise was flat as a pancake, dead as a doornail, dry as dust, and it couldn't have mattered less that she had her head on. The wedding dress they had wrapped her in was yellow and crusty and lay on her bones like a sail without a wind. Barren came to mind, but I dismissed it in favor of wafer-thin, translucent, light as a feather. For who's to say it wasn't she, after all, who had put away her sorry carcass and become the lightness of him who so weighed her down. Who's to say the time of her life hadn't at last begun?

# The Romance of Oxbridge:

# Virginia Woolf

Unable to contain her youthful rapture upon arriving in Oxford in the summer of 1914, Vera Brittain poured into her diary her "ecstatic entrancement":

> Oxford! What doesn't it call up to the mind! The greatest romance of England—the mellowed beauty of time and association, the finest lectures the world can produce, wonderful libraries and fascinating old bookshops . . .—oh God, have pity on my fierce excitement and grant that it may come to pass and be even better than I dream![1]

Toward the end of *To the Lighthouse* (1927), Cam Ramsay betrays a more composed but equally touching confidence in patriarchal English culture:

> Small as it was, and shaped something like a leaf stood on its end with the gold-sprinkled waters flowing in and about it, it had, she supposed, a place in the universe—even that little island? The old gentlemen in the study she thought could have told her. Sometimes she strayed in from the garden purposely to catch them at it. There they were (it might be Mr. Carmichael or Mr. Bankes who was sitting with her father) sitting opposite each other in their low arm-chairs. They were crackling in front of them the pages of *The Times*, when she came in from the garden, all in a muddle, about something some one had said about Christ, or hearing that a mammoth had been dug up in a London street, or wondering what Napoleon was like. Then they took all this with their clean hands (they wore grey-coloured clothes; they smelt of heather) and they brushed the scraps together, turning the paper, crossing their knees, and said something now and

then very brief. Just to please herself she would take a book from the shelf and stand there, watching her father write, so equally, so neatly from one side of the page to another, with a little cough now and then, or something said briefly to the other old gentleman opposite. And she thought, standing there with her book open, one could let whatever one thought expand here like a leaf in water; and if it did well here, among the old gentlemen smoking and *The Times* crackling then it was right. [2]

Like so many daughters and sisters of Oxbridge men, the youthful Virginia Woolf shared Cam's confidence in old gentlemen smoking and *The Times* crackling, but, like Vera Brittain, Woolf outlived it. By *Three Guineas* (1938) Woolf is writing of the old gentlemen in a different tone: "To fight has always been the man's habit, not the woman's."[3] Woolf's shift in tone from the early twenties to the late thirties marks her reluctant progress toward a conviction that the educated men of her own class and culture are responsible for war and that she must secure her mind and body against them if she is to survive. Her progress is reluctant because she adores patriarchal English culture, she loves her father, husband, and brothers, and she is extremely fond of several other Oxbridge men, but war (in retrospect and in prospect) forces her to painful conclusions.

Perhaps because Woolf stayed married, however oddly, to Leonard until she died and wrote him last words which certainly sound trusting and grateful, we tend to underestimate the extent to which she came to regard educated men as dangerous to herself, her sex, and the human race. Though we acknowledge Woolf's Oxbridge characters to be egoists, we take comfort in their resemblance to Meredith's Willoughby, an egoist whose impact on women and children is more comic than fatal. Mr. Ramsay is a bully, of course, but not the brute of a daddy who haunts Sylvia Plath's post–World War II imagination, not

The boot in the face, the brute
Brute heart of a brute like you. [4]

Woolf killed herself, we say, because she was mad, or about to be mad, or about to be forced to take the cure for her madness, omitting from our account the fact that she also chose death over living through the war which would breed in Sylvia Plath such self-annihilating cynicism on the subject of men and their habits.[5]

Though the elegiac *Jacob's Room* (1922) presents Oxbridge men more as victims than as purveyors of war and Woolf fears less their power than their power to prevail, by the time the Great War is a decade in the past and the next war a decade in the future, Woolf has grown more ambivalent. *A Room of One's Own* (1928) is a triumphant appropriation for women of the Oxbridge culture Woolf loved, periodically invaded by dark broodings on the connections between that culture, the men who produced it, and war. Still, in 1928, war seemed over rather than endemic, and Woolf could sustain enough confidence in English culture to operate on the premise that educated men can be moved by gentle chaffing or, at worst, inattention. *A Room of One's Own* treats us to the Oxbridge man at high table. The luncheon is too lavish and we wonder at his presumption of worthiness, but we are not obliged to view the carnage required to fill his plate. As in Ben Jonson's "To Penshurst," the fruits leap to the table as if impelled by their own eagerness to be consumed, and even when we come to weigh the cost, it is against the prunes and custard of Fernham, lowly fare and a violation, perhaps, to the spirit, but not to the body. Similarly, the flapping Beadle kills a thought,[6] but he poses no threat to life or limb. Sir Chartres Biron may be concealed behind the red curtain, but if so he is the old fool Polonius, not one of his more dangerous countrymen (*ROOO* 85). Vanity, not brutality, inspires these men, and in 1928 Woolf still believes that vain men can be moved by drawing their attention to the bald spots in the backs of their heads. Bristling with confidence in the educability of educated men, Woolf means in *A Room of One's Own* to tease them out of their bad habits.

But a darker view of the security of her own sex and the malleability of Oxbridge men asserts itself early in the text: "When the guns fired in August 1914, did the faces of men and women show so plain in each other's eyes that romance was killed? Certainly it was a shock (to women in particular with their illusions about education, and so on) to see the faces of our rulers in the light of the shell-fire" (*ROOO* 31). Among the old gentlemen smelling of heather, the light of the shell-fire reveals Professor von X snapping the pages of his monumental tome, *The Mental, Moral, and Physical Inferiority of the Female Sex.* To be sure, Professor von X is not an English gentleman and scholar. He is a German gentleman and scholar, and perhaps his war guilt enables Woolf to admit a horror she cannot bear to feel for the men of her own nation and class. Certainly, Woolf's portrait of the German scholar is severe, his face shockingly plain in the midst of her forgiving, occasionally even fond, delineations of Oxbridge men.

> He was not in my picture a man attractive to women. He was heavily built; he had a great jowl; to balance that he had very small eyes; he was very red in the face. His expression suggested that he was labouring under some emotion that made him jab his pen on the paper as if he were killing some noxious insect as he wrote, but even when he had killed it that did not satisfy him; he must go on killing it; and even so, some cause for anger and irritation remained. (*ROOO* 31)

Even in a German gentleman and scholar, Woolf cannot endure this unnerving recognition of a habit of killing for long, and she quickly swerves from her outrage to his: "Soon my own anger was explained and done with; but curiosity remained. How explain the anger of the professors? Why were they angry?" (*ROOO* 32). Only with this swerve from her rage and repugnance to a disinterested curiosity about his, can Woolf allow a resemblance between German professors and professors in general, between Professor von X and the father whose equal and neat letters are so reassuring to Cam.

Romance, that tendency of each sex to soften the features of the other, is not altogether dead in A *Room of One's Own,* nor is Virginia Woolf's own more intimate romance with Oxbridge's best and brightest, but both are under fire. Clearly, the daughter of an educated English man places her confidence in German gentlemen and scholars at her peril, but may she not trust the gentlemen who frequent her own drawing room, may she not enjoy in their company that enlightening and liberating confidence Cam so enjoyed among her father and his friends? In the speculations that arise from her reading of Mr. A.'s novel, Woolf comes dangerously close to recognizing the fascist in her own Bloomsbury circle and to concluding that to survive as a woman and a writer she must resist all the flowers of Oxbridge, but she swerves once again, this time to Italy.

> I began to envisage an age to come of pure, of self-assertive virility, such as the letters of professors (take Sir Walter Raleigh's letters, for instance) seem to forbode, and the rulers of Italy have already brought into being. For one can hardly fail to be impressed in Rome by the sense of unmitigated masculinity; and whatever the value of unmitigated masculinity upon the state, one may question the effect of it upon the art of poetry. At any rate, according to the newspapers, there is a certain anxiety about fiction in Italy. There has been a meeting of academicians whose object it is "to develop the Italian novel." "Men famous by birth, or in finance, industry or the Fascist corporations" came together the other day and discussed the matter, and a telegram was sent to the Duce expressing the hope "that the Fascist era would soon give birth to a poet worthy of it." We may all join the pious hope, but it is doubtful whether poetry can come out of an incubator. Poetry ought to have a mother as well as a father. The Fascist poem, one fears, will be a horrid little abortion such as one sees in a glass jar in the museum of some country town. (*ROOO* 106–7)

Woolf has been accused of finding the quality of masculinity distasteful, but in truth she finds it dangerous to both life and literature, and she acknowledges much more readily its prevalence abroad than its prevalence at home.

Still, a sense of personal danger does infuse the image of the horrid little abortion precisely because the locus of mutilation is the female body and the agents of mutilation are educated men. Superficially breezy in tone, *A Room of One's Own* is littered with somber reminders of the uses to which the female body has been put by educated men. In the service of his self-respect,

Professor von X must kill the noxious insect and kill it again. In the service of his art, the California movie director must lower the bedizened female body from a peak and hang it suspended in mid-air (*ROOO* 33). Nick Greene, a literary English gentleman, might have nurtured the literary genius of Shakespeare's sister, but he chose instead to get her pregnant. Betrayed by the creativity of her female body, Judith Shakespeare prefers death to incubating the horrid little abortion of a gentleman who likes to say that a woman acting puts him in mind of a dog dancing. Nowhere in *A Room of One's Own* does Woolf openly express fear for her own body or mind in the hands of the educated English men she knows, yet her choice of a name for her persona hints of an unacknowledged dread. "Call me Mary Beton, Mary Seton, Mary Carmichael or by any name you please" (*ROOO* 5), the persona of *A Room of One's Own* says in an aside to the reader. The three Marys figure in an old English ballad narrated by a fourth, Mary Hamilton, who is awaiting execution for bearing the king's child. The opening lines of the ballad succinctly pronounce her doom: "Last night there were four Marys, Tonight there will be but three." Since each of the three Marys appears in Woolf's text—Mary Seton presides over custard and prunes at Fernham; Mary Beton provides the legacy which, to her niece, is so infinitely more important than the vote; Mary Carmichael writes the novel in which Chloe likes Olivia—we can assume that Woolf takes the name—and the fate?—of the fourth Mary to be her own.

Though the vulnerability of her female body and its products to the predations of educated men is a source of dark foreboding to Woolf, she is not prepared to conclude in 1928 that the men she knows and the literature she loves are leading to war or to her own bodily or literary mutilation. The final chapter of *A Room of One's Own* opens with the charming romance of a man and woman approaching from opposite ends of a street to step into a taxi cab together.

The sight was ordinary enough; what was strange was the rhythmical order with which my imagination had invested it, and the fact that the ordinary sight of two people getting into a cab had the power to communicate something of their own seeming satisfaction. The sight of two people coming down the street and meeting at the corner seems to ease the mind of some strain, I thought, watching the taxi turn and make off. Perhaps to think, as I had been thinking these two days, of one sex as distinct from the other is an effort. It interferes with the unity of the mind. Now that effort had ceased and that unity had been restored by seeing two people come together and get into a taxi-cab. (*ROOO* 100–101)

Woolf still hopes for amity between herself and Oxbridge; mutual friendship between educated English women and men still seems to her the best way to prevent war and to succor the products of her own mind and body. But the comfort of seeing the couple enter the cab, and the comfort of discovering the woman in Shakespeare and the woman in Coleridge soon dissipate under the pressure of rows and rows of novels by Kipling and Galsworthy, and Woolf is driven to conclude:

Some of the finest works of our greatest living writers fall upon deaf ears. Do what she will a woman cannot find in them that fountain of perpetual life which the critics assure her is there. It is not only that they celebrate male virtues, enforce male values and describe the world of men; it is that the emotion with which these books are permeated is to a woman incomprehensible. (*ROOO* 105–6)

The rift between the sexes, momentarily bridged by the couple's entrance into the cab, gapes wide again the moment Woolf encounters in Oxbridge men and their products the emotions that lead to and serve war. In a work that presumes the educability of educated men, however, this intuition of an unbreachable divide between the sexes is bound to be suppressed. Though despair is an undercurrent in A *Room of One's Own*, it is a response less to the inaccessibility of the male mind than to the accessibility of the female body. Woolf's pessimism about the consequences for women of sexual intercourse with educated men is balanced by her optimism about the consequences of a marriage of minds. "Some collaboration has to take place in the mind between the woman and the man before the act of creation can be accomplished. Some marriage of opposites has to be consummated. The whole of the mind must lie wide open if we are to get the sense that the writer is communicating his experience with perfect fullness" (*ROOO* 108). Familiar as she is with the fates of Judith Shakespeare and Mary Hamilton, that Woolf should posit so biological a model of creativity bespeaks an extraordinary need for confidence in educated men, a need not balked by the fact that the language of educated men cannot express it. In the King's English, of course, need, like every other human experience, is his to communicate, and we already know the cost to her of lying wide open to the king.

By 1937, the nuptials between Woolf and Oxbridge are off, and we hear no more talk of lying wide open to educated men. History is about to confirm what Woolf most fears, that educated English men are leading their daughters, sisters, and wives yet again to war. As early as March 1936, Woolf records in her diary the relentless approach of the guns: "Its odd, how near the guns have got to our private life again. I can quite distinctly see them and hear a roar, even though I go on, like a doomed mouse, nibbling at my daily page."[7] The guns come still closer in July 1937, when Woolf's nephew Julian is killed while driving an ambulance in Spain. Woolf had argued strenuously against Julian's resolve to enlist in the Spanish Civil War and *Three Guineas* is, in part, an effort to legitimize a response other than guns to a legitimate cause. In the memoir she prepares shortly after Julian's death, Woolf writes: "Though I understand that this is a 'cause', can be called the cause of liberty & so on, still my natural reaction is to fight intellectually: if I were any use, I should write against it: I should evolve some plan for fighting English tyranny. The moment force is used, it becomes meaningless and unreal to me."[8] But being of use in a literary rather than a military way is less on Woolf's mind, I think, than the heavy weight of her own and her sister's grief and of the prospect of war. *Three Guineas* is an escape from intolerable personal emotions, and one that affords Woolf extraordinary pleasure and relief. She calls the book her "happy tumultuous dream" (*D* 5:52), her "magic bubble" (*D* 5:101). It is the thin wall between herself and "the pale disillusioned world" (D 5:101), the grass plot "just on tother side" of "immeasurable despair" (D 5:102). It is a grass plot upon which Woolf walks, however, with "energy and delight" (D 5:102), upon which she even has several good gallops (D 5:65, 112).

That *Three Guineas*, despite its severity of subject and tone, should give Woolf such pleasure in a time of such misery is a measure of her compulsion to write it. "But I want—how violently, how persistently, pressingly compulsorily I cant say—to write this book" (D 5:133), she admits to her diary. Temporarily put aside, *Three Guineas* "flames up" in Woolf again the evening she spends discussing with her nephew, Stephen Spender, and Kingsley Martin "hand grenades, bombs, tanks, as if we were military gents in the war again" (D 5:80). As she nears the conclusion of the first draft, she not only gallops but erupts: "Oh how violently I have been galloping through these mornings! It has pressed & spurted out of me, if that's any proof of virtue, like a physical volcano. And my brain feels cool & quiet after the expulsion" (D 5:112). What fuels the book, finally, is Woolf's joy at expressing openly, without the element of charm, her abhorrence of war and of the patriarchal culture which inspires, fosters, and celebrates war. *Three Guineas* is as forbidding to Oxbridge men as *A Room of One's Own* was inviting, and its chastity marks the progress of Woolf's alienation from dear old English gentlemen and dear old English culture. The shell-fire which, in *A Room of One's Own*, lit up Professor von X, now discloses "Man himself," a figure far more inclusive than his specifically German prototype:

> It is the figure of a man; some say, others deny, that he is Man himself, the quintessence of virility, the perfect type of which all the others are imperfect adumbrations. He is a man certainly. His eyes are glazed; his eyes glare. His body, which is braced in an unnatural position, is tightly cased in a uniform. Upon the breast of that uniform are sewn several medals and other mystic symbols. His hand is upon a sword. He is called in German and Italian Fuhrer or Duce; in our own language Tyrant or Dictator. And behind him lie ruined houses and dead bodies—men, women and children. (TG 142)

Unlike Professor von X, this quintessence of man has a name in the English language and a place in English culture; his presence will be revealed from Oxbridge to Whitehall, from Wimpole Street to Bloomsbury. Unlike the Oxbridge men at high table, this quintessence of man is not granted a saving distance between his private pleasures and their far-reaching human costs, costs measured now not in custard and prunes but in ruined houses and dead bodies.

Such a figure of the educated man invites not gentle chaffing but resistance. "Where is it leading us," Woolf demands in *Three Guineas*, "the procession of educated men?" (62). And she answers, emphatically and repeatedly, to photographs like these:

> Here then on the table before us are photographs. The Spanish Government sends them with patient pertinacity about twice a week. They are not pleasant photographs to look upon. They are photographs of dead bodies for the most part. This morning's collection contains the photograph of what might be a man's body, or a woman's; it is so mutilated that it might, on the other hand, be the body of a pig. But those certainly are dead children, and that undoubtedly is the section of a house. A bomb has torn open the side; there is still a bird-cage hanging in what was presumably the sitting-room; but the rest of the house looks like nothing so much as a bunch of spilikins suspended in mid-air. (*TG* 10–11)

Recognition of the carnage educated men strew about them leads Woolf to conclude by 1937 that their daughters, sisters, and wives had best steel their bodies, minds, and hearts against them.

Woolf's conclusion is starkly reflected in her grammar. The frame of *Three Guineas* is a letter from *us* in response to a query from *you* as to how to prevent war. Inset in that frame are two letters to women in which the pronoun references vary, but when addressing a man Woolf sharply and consistently divides *you* from *us*. "You," she explains early on,

> are a little grey in the temples; the hair is no longer thick on the top of your head. You have reached the middle years of life, not without effort, at the Bar; but on the whole your journey has been prosperous. There is nothing parched, mean or dissatisfied in your

expression. And without wishing to flatter you, your prosperity—wife, children, house—has been deserved. You have never sunk into the contented apathy of middle life, for, as your letter from an office in the heart of London shows, instead of turning on your pillow and prodding your pigs, pruning your pear trees—you have a few acres in Norfolk—you are writing letters, attending meetings, presiding over this and that, asking questions, with the sound of the guns in your ears. For the rest, you began your education at one of the great public schools and finished it at the university. (TG 3–4)

Addressed throughout in a tone of affectionate familiarity, this promising specimen of the Oxbridge man seems to have little in common with Tyrants or Dictators, with ruined houses or mutilated bodies. But it is always the point of *Three Guineas* to trace the connection between the private brother and the public warmonger, to expose the process by which patriarchal institutions

sink the private brother, whom many of us have reason to respect, and inflate in his stead a monstrous male, loud of voice, hard of fist, childishly intent upon scoring the floor of the earth with chalk marks, within whose mystic boundaries human beings are penned, rigidly, separately, artificially; where, daubed red and gold, decorated like a savage with feathers he goes through mystic rites and enjoys the dubious pleasures of power and dominion while we, "his" women, are locked in the private house without share in the many societies of which his society is composed. (TG 105)

Grammatically, *Three Guineas* reflects this inflationary process by continuously transposing the generic *you* (educated English men) upon the specific *you* (middle-aged balding man with wife, children, house, and a few acres in Norfolk). Close attention to Woolf's discussion of Arthur's Education Fund (TG 4–5) reveals clearly this tendency of *you* to conflate the individual man with the patriarchal collective. As winning as the Oxbridge man may be as a brother or an intimate, he cannot escape the consequences of the exclusionary laws and customs he has practiced and profited by. Though Woolf posits from time to time a society in which men and women are not so sharply divided, she is always conscious of writing from within one in which the division has been so rigorously enforced that "though we look at the same things, we see them differently" (*TG* 5).

While *you* in the frame letter means now a man, then Man himself, *we* remains anonymously and collectively female, referring always to any English woman with a mind of her own. But as Woolf details what an English woman requires to have a mind of her own under the Crown, *our* numbers steadily dwindle. A structural battle between the sexes is waged in *Three Guineas*, which results in you men being everywhere, we women being nowhere, outside and invisible.

While masculine discourse pins woman to her sex, allowing her to speak for herself or her sex but never for men and women alike, in the inset letters addressed to women, *you* and *us* intermingle. Released from the impact of the "monstrous male . . . scoring the floor of the earth with chalk marks, within whose mystic boundaries human beings are penned, rigidly, separately, artificially" (*TG* 105), feminine discourse encourages an erosion of boundaries, permitting a collaboration between *you* and *us* rather than the absorption of *us* by *you*. The flexibility of the pronouns in discourse among women underscores their intransigence in discourse between the sexes, and suggests the depth of Woolf's disillusionment with her romance of androgyny.

Woolf's relinquishment of her biological metaphor of creativity and her relocation of her creative energies within a community of women allows her, finally, to abandon the educated man. A *Room of One's Own*'s receptive language of marriage and creative intercourse gives way, in *Three Guineas*, to a language of divorce and embattlement. Its appeal to the educated man is ironic; it will advise women to close their ears to him and listen to each other.

Abandoning the educated man is as consistent with the logic as with the grammar of *Three Guineas*, both of which require, above all, the preservation of his sister's difference from him. "Any help we can give you," Woolf says early in the text, "must be different from that you give yourselves, and the value of that help may be in the fact of that difference" (*TG* 18). Her argument concludes less tentatively: "But as a result the answer to your question must be that we can best help you prevent war not by repeating your words and following your methods but by finding new words and creating new methods. We can best help you prevent war not by joining your society but by remaining outside your society but in co-operation with its aims" (TG 143). Woolf is aware of the paradox at the heart of her argument. Like a monstrous male childishly scoring the earth, she must pen in her sex if she is to preserve women from the habits of mind and discourse that lead to war. Beleaguered an enclave as they are, educated women with minds different from those of their fathers and brothers seem to Woolf, in 1937, the last bulwark against war. With the stakes so high, the categorical distinction must be preserved.

That, by 1937, Woolf feels endangered, personally and collectively, is evident in both the structure and the texture of *Three Guineas*. As the vast web of trenches along the front lines of World War I speaks graphically of the physical perils of the men who inhabited them, so the excessively elaborated structure of *Three Guineas* (its letters within letters, its footnotes, its obsessive symmetries) bears the imprint of an imperiled mind. Woolf defines the danger to her mind in the language of her body. As Isa, in *Between the Acts* (1941), recognizes the connection between her fear of her husband and a newspaper account of the gang rape of a young woman by troopers at Whitehall,[9] so Woolf in *Three Guineas* insists on the connection between rape of the mind and rape of the body, urging women to value and defend their minds with the same passion as they have been trained to value and defend their bodies. Advising women to practice chastity of the mind, Woolf warns them against "adultery of the brain" (TG 93) and a "prostituted culture" (TG 95). That model of healthy intercourse between the sexes that Woolf entertained in *A Room of One's Own* gives way, under the pressure of yet another war, to a model of contamination and molestation.

The most virulent public outbreaks of the disease of unmitigated masculinity take the form of war, the most virulent private outbreaks take the form of tyrannical fatherhood. Fathers particularly frighten Woolf in 1937, perhaps because she has outlived her sexual vulnerability. Certainly Woolf's own father bore down hard on her after the death of his wife, but Woolf's fear is not of Leslie Stephens. Her fear is rooted in the crucial recognition of the text—that the Fuhrer, the Duce, the Tyrant, the Dictator are bred in the private house. Woolf documents at length the driving passion of certain fathers, unchecked by any social or legal constraints, to keep their daughters in their power, citing the examples of Mr. Barrett, Rev. Patrick Brontë, and Mr. Jex-Blake, and quoting profusely from *The Report of the Archbishop's Commission on the Ministry of Women*. In *A Room of One's Own*, Woolf takes as her emblem the condemned Mary Hamilton; in *Three Guineas* she chooses the condemned Antigone. While Mary Hamilton is executed for having the king's baby, Antigone is buried alive for daring to differ with her uncle.

Though they do not bury her alive, neither the fathers nor the sons of Woolf's Bloomsbury circle welcome the book that erupts so violently from her. E. M. Forster, who found "the charming and persuasive" *A Room of One's Own* to be "one of the most brilliant of her books," pronounces "the cantankerous *Three Guineas*" to be "the worst of her books." Its "extreme Feminism," he diagnoses rather wistfully as "old-fashioned": "It dates back to her suffragette youth of the 1910s, when men kissed girls to distract them from wanting the vote, and very properly provoked her wrath. By the 1930s she had much less to complain of, and seems to keep on grumbling from habit."[10] Forster overlooks, of course, Woolf's chief complaint in 1936—that educated English men are leading their daughters, wives, and sisters once again to war. The sons of Bloomsbury, who might have to fight the war, do not, but they think it unseemly that Woolf should link her complaint against war with her complaint against men. Quentin Bell, in his biography of his aunt, recalls his own anger at the book when it appeared in 1938:

> What really seemed wrong with the book, and I am speaking here of my own reactions at the time—was the attempt to involve a discussion of women's rights with the far more agonizing and immediate question of what we were to do in order to meet the ever-growing menace of Fascism and war. The connection between the two ques-

tions seemed tenuous and the positive suggestions wholly inadequate. (VWB 205)

Forster's and Quentin Bell's are not Bloomsbury's most heated responses to *Three Guineas*. Bell recalls that "Maynard Keynes was both angry and contemptuous; it was, he declared, a silly argument and not very well written" (VWB 205). What both fathers and sons of Bloomsbury cannot abide are the connections Woolf insists upon between men, women, and war. Bell cannot hear the menace of Fascism in his own voice when he so instinctively grants priority to his own sex, and it doesn't occur to Forster that a feminist might make a significant contribution to a debate about how to prevent war.

Woolf feels the temperatures rising around her. News of Maynard Keynes's anger reaches her before she actually encounters him in August 1938. She is nervous about the meeting, gives herself a talking to in her diary: "Now the thing to remember is that I'm an independent & perfectly established human being: no one can bully me: & at the same time nothing shall make me shrivel into a martyr or a bitter persecution maniac" (D 5:163). When the meeting finally occurs, Maynard doesn't say a word about the book. "Dear old Hitler" (D 5:163), Woolf calls him, recognizing at last the fascist in her own drawing room. She is less troubled by the heat, however, than by the coolness of her friends' reactions to the book. Many are silent, even Leonard doesn't seem to really like it: "I didn't get so much praise from L. as I hoped," Woolf writes in her diary after his first reading of *Three Guineas*.

Considerably less adverse criticism had broken Woolf's confidence in her work in the past. Her diary records a bitter struggle to keep faith in *The Years*. Oddly, neither the heat nor the coolness of Bloomsbury to *Three Guineas* seems to seriously undermine her confidence and satisfaction in the book. She does care that Philippa Strachey, a feminist, likes the book: "I felt if I had written all that & it was not to her liking I should have to brace myself pretty severely in my own private esteem" (D 5:147). She doesn't care that Queenie Leavis doesn't. She is prepared for attacks from women as well as from men, and rightly judges this one to be "personal" (*D* 5:165). *Three Guineas* seems to give Woolf a clarity of vision about the relation of "Man himself" to his more familiar manifestations as father, brother, husband, and friend, which toughens her against attack and indifference. Though she doesn't think *Three Guineas* will prevent World War II, she does feel she has made an original and important contribution to the effort to prevent it. After the book has been out three months and most of the reactions are in, she writes in her diary: "I feel I said what I wanted in 3 Gs & am not to care if its 1: made my own friends hostile; laid me open to abuse and ridicule; also praise where I don't want it; & paying bills for Wms. Societies: 3.9 for a ridiculous leaflet—that's my debt to civilization" (*D* 5:170).

*Men Are Like That*, Woolf initially called *Three Guineas* (*D* 4:77), driving a stake between *you* and *us*, between Oxbridge men and their daughters, sisters, and wives. The more reticent *Three Guineas* exposes less, but its import is the same (as Woolf's contemporaries recognized when they called it her *Lysistrata*)— if a woman is to have a mind of her own and use it to prevent war, she must keep it clear of the minds of her father, husband, and brothers. With World War II all but inevitable, Woolf's romance of Oxbridge succumbs to her romance of the Outsider's Society, her desire to get in becoming a determination to get out, her aspiration to man-womanliness transforming into a crusade to get the man out of woman. Today, the irony of Woolf's last romance is painfully apparent. The procession of educated men has not been checked, war now has no outside, and no woman on earth is beyond the arms of educated men.

## NOTES

1. Vera Brittain, *Testament of Youth* (New York, 1980), 63–64.
2. Virginia Woolf, *To the Lighthouse* (New York, 1957), 281–82. Hereafter referred to as *TTL*.
3. Virginia Woolf, *Three Guineas* (New York, 1938), 6. Hereafter referred to as *TG*.

4. Sylvia Plath, *Ariel* (New York, 1965), 50. Mr. Ramsay's boots are, in fact, more consoling than terrifying, as Lily Briscoe discovers when she praises his boots in lieu of solacing his soul (*TTL* 228–30).

5. A *New York Times Book Review* article on the fifth and final volume of Virginia Woolf's diaries reveals that Virginia and Leonard Woolf kept a can of petrol in the garage "for the purpose of committing suicide by carbon monoxide poisoning" if Hitler won the war or invaded England ("Virginia Woolf: Great Miseries and Great Joys," July 29, 1984, 32).

6. Virginia Woolf, *A Room of One's Own* (New York, 1957), 6. Hereafter referred to as *ROOO*.

7. *The Diary of Virginia Woolf*, ed. Anne Olivier Bell with Andrew McNeillie, 5 vols. (London: Hogarth, 1977–84), 5:17. Hereafter referred to as *D*.

8. Quentin Bell, *Virginia Woolf: A Biography* (New York, 1972), 258–59. Hereafter referred to as *VWB*.

9. Virginia Woolf, *Between the Acts* (London, 1941), 27.

10. S. P. Rosenbaum, ed., *The Bloomsbury Group* (Toronto, 1975), 215.

# Little Women

It had been a long day, disposing of the family. I wasn't happy about packing up my house and my father, and I had listened all morning to my mother's sour stories about the silver spoons in the buffet drawer my father bought his mother with his choirboy money, and the brand new nylons still in their wrappers my father bought his mother during the war. I found them in your grandmother's bureau after she died, my mother told me. Edna wouldn't wear them during the war because they cost too much, and afterward, they were too ugly.

So I was glad to escape for the afternoon into the attic, and when I unearthed, behind a trunk full of my father's uniforms and war relics, the doll he brought home from the war for me, I picked it up and turned it over and, as in an hourglass, time ran back and I heard first the faint honk of a duck and then the steady beat of wings on water and then I am there, sitting on the kitchen floor in the house on Seneca Lake. We are still in the navy, so my father can't have been home very long. He is a stranger to me and I shiver when his shadow falls on me. The doll he has brought me from Brazil has a tiny waist and a huge ruffled taffeta skirt and a basket on her head with bananas and grapes and a pineapple in it. My mother scolds him for the bananas and grapes and the pineapple. Don't you know, she says, they put everything in their mouths. Then she says, Of course you don't know, and they don't say anything after that so they both hear me gasp when I turn the doll upside down and lo and behold underneath the skirt is another tiny waist, another head with a basket of bananas and grapes and a pineapple in it. They both laugh then but not so loud that they don't hear me whisper to my mother, Where does she grow her babies? and then they both laugh harder and I get mad and throw the doll across the room and howl. Dorothy, he says, like my mother is to blame and that makes me feel better but it makes her get up and leave the room. What am I supposed to do, my father says to no one in particular and then he gets up and leaves too, so I retrieve the doll and sit in the chair where my mother would be if my father hadn't come home from the war, and I turn the doll over and over again.

I am still turning her over when my father comes back with a gun and starts shooting ducks out the kitchen window. Boom, the gun goes like thunder, and the cartridge skitters across the floor and I turn the doll over to see if she still has her other head on. Boom, the gun goes again and the cartridge slides across the floor when Boom my mother comes in and says, God damn your eyes, and grabs the gun and Boom the gun goes again and glass falls like rain and my mother snatches me and the doll up from the chair and she throws the doll at my father and she says, God damn your eyes and your guns and your Brazilian whore, and that was the last I saw of the doll until that afternoon when we were disposing of the family.

The doll was wrapped in foil like a tulip bulb, and next to it lay the little women dolls we got the Christmas Katie was eleven and I was nine and we were living in the house we were disposing of that day, and there hadn't been any guns around for years. I wasn't surprised when Katie got Jo. Katie never climbed trees or helped Dad with the storm windows or wanted to run away to the navy, but she got Jo because she was older. I got Beth who was always dying. Aunt Carol sent Amy to us both. I was hoping for Meg, Katie might trade Beth and my half of Meg for Jo, but Amy wasn't worth much to either one of us. I was putting up a good front, laying Beth out on the sofa with a wet towel on her forehead like her sisters always did when she had a headache, when I noticed a packet at the bottom of the box Amy came in. Inside were three tiny, hand-knit bikinis—green for Jo, blue for Beth, pink for Amy—and three identically colored, hand-knit ice-skating outfits with matching hats, mittens, and socks.

How, I said to my mother, did she ever find time to make them? My mother never had time for doll clothes or Halloween costumes or cookies for the class Valentine's Day party.

Oh look, my mother said, they come with their own curlers. And, indeed, they did. Jo, Beth, and Amy each had a little grooming kit with a comb, a mirror, and six tiny pink rubber curlers like six short, fat worms.

I pretended to be too busy with Beth's curlers to notice that my mother hadn't answered my question. I was sorry as soon as I asked it. Carol was, of course, having another baby. Katie and I were ecstatic about the first one, a little cousin we could take for walks in a baby carriage at the shore, but the little cousin never came. A miscarriage, my mother called it, and Katie and I agreed we must be to blame. We were relieved several months later to hear Carol was having another, but then we overheard Mother telling Dad how sick Carol was and how she had been in bed for months. She sent us each an afghan that time. The third time Carol was having a baby, Katie and I each gave up our favorite food—no gum balls for me, no chocolate-covered marshmallow cookies for Katie—but Carol arrived a few months later looking ten years older and still without a baby of her own. Katie said Carol was divorcing Uncle Tom because he killed her babies but Tom was my favorite uncle so I said it had something to do with the war. After a month and a half, Carol went home and now it was Christmas and she was having a baby again.

I snatched Beth up from the sofa where she was reclining and stripped her of her long dress and pantaloons. She looked alive in her tiny blue bikini and I was teaching her to jack knife off the sofa into a pool of blue tissue paper when Katie stood up, stamped her foot, and said, He's making her have another baby.

My father was gone by then, I don't know where he found

to go on Christmas morning in Plainfield, New Jersey, but I remember he said there were too many little women for him and
he'd be back in a while. He isn't making her have a baby,
mother shouted from the kitchen where she was frying bacon.
It takes two to tango.

I told you, I said to Katie, I told you it was the war.

My mother had turned off the bacon and was standing in
the doorway looking at me. It was the war, she said, but then
my father came home and I never remembered to ask her what
we meant.

So I carried Jo downstairs where mother was sitting on the
bed she and Dad used to sleep in. On her lap was a photograph of my father with the shark he caught deep-sea fishing
off the Jersey coast the summer I was ten. I put the doll in her
lap next to the photograph. Why couldn't Carol have babies
because of the war? I said. Mother looked up at me, then
down at the doll and the photograph, and then she began to
speak, slowly at first, as though sifting the debris of a still
smouldering house for the one momento she couldn't afford to
lose.

From the moment your father's mother arrived at the shore
that summer of '45, every other word out of her mouth was
your father's name. Doesn't Austen look fine in his uniform?
Won't Austen be ashamed that Katie is such a cry baby? Did I
ever see the silver spoons Austen bought with his choirboy
money? And shouldn't I be thanking my lucky star for snagging
a husband like Austen, instead of out drinking with the coast
guard? I never even called him Austen, I hated the name.

Edna's bureau was an altar to the son she had named after
her brother: Austen in his choir robe, his varsity swimming
sweater, his mortarboard, his uniform, his intern's shirt, his
wedding suit, Austen with his arm around his sister, Austen
with a daughter on each knee.

Carol shrank to a shadow, I hardly knew her. Every morning Edna would say, Run by the post office, Carol, and see if
there's a letter from Austen. And Carol would slip off without a

murmur about how she had a husband of her own on an air-craft carrier in a much hotter spot than Rio de Janeiro.

One day in early June we were trudging home from the beach in the mid-day heat for the heavy German dinner Edna made us eat every day at noon. You girls were complaining every inch of the way and we had to get the tar off your feet and the sand out of your hair and put you in clean clothes, then you sat at the table pushing your chicken and dumplings and peas around on your plates until I said you could be excused. Austen would make them sit at the table until they cleaned their plates, Edna said. He'll have his hands full when he gets home.

No fuller than they are now, I said. What with his residency and his specialization and his this and his that, I don't suppose he'll have my girls on his hands much more than he does now.

He would if you had a boy, Edna said. Austen was so sure the second would be a boy. At least.

I left the room but I hung around outside the door to see if Carol would say anything. She didn't.

The next morning, Carol got up early and brewed the strong coffee Edna always said would surely give her a heart attack. Carol was drinking a cup alone at the kitchen table when I came in to warm up some milk. Here's to you, she raised her cup and grinned the way she used to at the Shore Hotel. Then Carol put down her cup and walked into her mother's room and I watched her take the suitcase from under the bed where Edna was still sleeping, and silently and properly pack her mother up. She didn't miss a thimble or a garter or a corset lace. Edna's voluminous underclothing was still on the line, damp in the morning dew. Carol unpinned the corsets, the thick stockings, the chemises, the underpants like tents, folded them neatly and wrapped them in wax paper. The snap of the suitcase lid and the click of the clasps roused Edna at last. What do you think you're doing? she said as she sat straight up, her iron gray hair swaying like a horsetail down her back.

You're going, Mother, Carol said. It's you or us and there

are four of us with no place to go. So you get yourself
dressed, Mother. You're leaving on the nine o'clock train.
There's coffee in the kitchen if you want it, she paused at the
door to add.

When Carol came back from the station she was almost herself again. She gathered up the mountain of towels, blankets,
buckets, shovels, and snacks you and Katie required on the
beach, and she lined us all up, gave us each a bundle, and
barked, Over the top, girls.

We were surprised to see a crowd at the 27th Street beach.
Some days we looked the length of the beach and didn't see a
thing except the coast guard tower. Today there were jeeps and
guys in uniform milling around, even a few women and kids.
Jimbo was there with the parrot so we went to take a look.

Sharks, Jimbo said. I looked where he was pointing and
laughed out loud. It was like a cartoon, three tiny black sails
cutting through the waves a hundred yards out.

We're going to shoot them, Jimbo said and the parrot said,
Bombs away, and Carol said, Why not just stay out of the water? No sport in that, Jimbo called back as he loped toward the
rowboat his buddies were already shouldering through the surf.

The boat nearly tipped over twice before they got to the
sharks and it rocked wildly as they fell all over each other trying to get off a shot. For a minute the boat and the guns and
the sharks were kicking up so much water I couldn't see a
thing. I heard Jimbo hoot and the parrot caw and the sea gulls
shriek. Somebody shouted, Score, and things settled down and
I saw a shark floating belly up near the boat. Katie and you
wanted to watch them bring it in but Carol said you'd seen
enough. She said I'd seen enough, too.

We'd been camped on the beach more than an hour the
next day before you girls found the baby. Carol and I were talking about Edna and who was to blame and we didn't notice
you two drifting down the beach until Katie started yelling and
jumping around and waving her arms. She was a block down
the beach and I couldn't see you anywhere and I tore down the

sand like a bullet. There you were, lying on your belly next to a small shark, fingering the four holes in its side. Carol was right behind me. I will never have a boy, she said.

And she hasn't, my mother said, staring at Jo and the photograph on her lap. And neither have I.

I picked up Jo and started to leave. Sit down, my mother said. I'm not finished.

It's later that same summer, a morning in early August. It's as hot as hot can be and the sand burns your feet and the beach is full of people whose war is over. The radios are blaring big bands and Sinatra, the men are playing volleyball, you kids are getting used to getting out of their way, Carol and I are talking about what life will be like when our men come home. Suddenly Carol shivers. Somebody's walking on my grave, she says, and then the radios are silent until everybody notices something is missing and then all the radios are playing "God Bless America." The announcement is brief, everybody knows the war is over now but nobody cheers or even smiles. Somebody's digging our grave, I say.

I went back to the attic then, and put the doll from Brazil and the little women dolls and their bikinis and ice-skating outfits in a garbage bag. I knotted it at the top and toted it back and forth across the country for fifteen years, but I never opened it up until I had a daughter of my own ready, I thought, for the doll from Brazil. I unearthed the garbage bag from under the eaves of the first home I'd had since the one we disposed of that day so long ago. As I pulled out the doll and turned her over, over again that hourglass went, but where time stops now there are no ducks or wings on water, there's a sea of people and the muted whoosh of airplanes landing and taking off and I am sitting on a bench in Newark Airport with much too much blood coming from where that doll has her other head. I am afraid for the back of my skirt and I would get up and go to the ladies' room at the far end of the crowded waiting room except I am drowning here in a pool of blood.

I arranged for the abortion through a Chinese laundry in Jersey City. A friend of a friend had a phone number he told me to call and say, I can't get the blood out of my husband's blue silk shirt. At the Chinese laundry, I got another number to call, where I was told to bring seven hundred and fifty dollars in cash to Newark Airport where I'd be picked up by a woman in a white Impala with Yale and Princeton stickers on the rear window. I slept through the alarm the morning I was to fly from Ithaca to Newark and the plane was pulling away from the terminal when I arrived. I said my mother was dying and they stopped the plane and let me on.

The other white-faced girl in the back of the Impala was from Barnard and the fat jolly woman driver chattered on about college and our courses and our boyfriends as she wound through downtown Newark. She pulled up in front of an elegant high rise on the outskirts of the city. As we waited for the elevator, the woman pinched me and hissed, Don't look so scared. We walked off the elevator into a penthouse apartment full of furniture from Hong Kong. Relax, the woman said, and she counted our money and gave us each a pill and sent us to the bedroom to lie down.

Relax, I say to myself on the bench at Newark Airport but the blood keeps flowing and I am fighting for consciousness so I won't be hauled off in an ambulance and everyone will know. As the room spins, I fix my eyes on the Airport Lounge hovering near the ceiling where Dad took me for a Shirley Temple cocktail the afternoon we drove up to see the plane wreck in the Elizabeth River. And when the Airport Lounge is as thin as a cloud floating over a heaving sea, I hear again that woman say, Shut up or this kid will be your last. And then the Beatles are shrieking, I want to hold your hand, and then there is a scream, frail and distant as ice cracking in the pond I used to skate on as a girl, and then I hear, as if this alone is cause for regret, It's a boy. I'm slipping off the bench and I want to drown, but I'm snagged, hooked, something won't let me go. Hold on, a voice says so absolutely I think it is God's and I open my eyes and there is a woman and she looks like Aunt Carol and she says again, Hold on, and I do.

I put the little women dolls back under the eaves and wrapped up the doll from Brazil and gave her to my daughter for her third birthday. She cut her finger on a sliver of glass nestled among the bananas and grapes and the pineapple. I tried to take the doll away from her but she howled like I was cutting her in half, so I took it outside and shook it hard and now she is sitting on the kitchen floor turning it over and over and over again.

# To El Salvador:

# Joan Didion

Like abortion and childbirth, war is an experience men and women have not shared. For women, the battlefield is shrouded by the same sex mysteries and taboos that shroud the birth chamber from men. While European and American women novelists of the last two centuries have experienced and recorded in their fictions the effects of war, the war zone itself has remained a peculiarly alien masculine territory, akin to the locker room and the men's club, only more unthinkable. Even when Virginia Woolf in *Three Guineas* counsels women to avert their eyes from the warrior, her own eyes penetrate only to his trappings, not to his actual activities.

Since H. W. Garrod's essay on Jane Austen, in which the Oxford don chides "the mere slip of a girl" for trifling with matters of home while Napoleon burned Europe,[1] it has been common to regard women novelists' inattention to war as emblematic of their trivialization of human experience, of their deflection of attention from the important to the petty. When women writers refuse to imagine what goes on in war, however, they may do so not out of ignorance or humility but out of fear and loathing. Experiencing war only obliquely, they may be intensely reluctant to come any closer.

In novels by Colette and Rebecca West about the First World War, the war is present not as an experience but as the absence of one, as the empty space between two distinctly different structures of feeling, two sharply antagonistic views of Western men and their culture. Virginia Woolf offers the women of Newnham this model for comprehending the Great War when, in *A Room of One's Own*, she asks: "When the guns fired in August 1914, did the faces of men and women show so plain in each other's eyes that romance was killed? Certainly it was a shock (to women in particular with their illusions about education, and so on) to see the faces of our rulers in the light of the shell-fire."[2] In Colette's *Cheri* and *The Last of Cheri*, the Great War is literally the empty space between the two novels. *Cheri* concludes just before the outbreak of World War I; *The Last of Cheri* opens with Cheri telling at the dinner table the pathetic little war story he already knows by heart. Rebecca West, in *The Return of the Soldier*, evades the experience of war not only by opening with the soldier's homecoming, but also by bringing him home from the front shell-shocked, his memory of the last decade apparently utterly obliterated.

Vera Brittain, in *Testament of Youth*, seems not to share this reluctance to approach the battlefield. Having succeeded against terrific odds in following the brave young men to Oxford, she naturally wanted to follow them to greater fields of glory. Succeeding, again at great odds, in making her way to a hospital station some twenty miles behind the front lines, she was called home to nurse her hypochondriac mother. Her outrage at being dragged back to the protected zone is exceeded only by her outrage later on, when she comes to count her losses, that the experience of war should ever have been presented to her as compelling or ennobling. Devoting the rest of her life to the elimination of war from the face of the earth, Brittain comes to regard war's "allure" as its greatest danger:

> The causes of war are always falsely represented; its honour is dishonest and its glory meretricious, but the challenge to spiritual endurance, the intense sharpening of all the senses, the vitalizing consciousness of common peril for a common end, remain to allure those boys and girls who have just reached the age when love and friendship and adventure call more persistently than at any later time. The glamour may be the mere delirium of fever, which as soon as war is over dies out and shows itself for the will-o'-the-wisp that it

is, but while it lasts no emotion known to man seems as yet to have quite the compelling power of this enlarged vitality.[3]

Though several women novelists were swept away by romantic emotions to the First World War, most of their fictions of the postwar period delineate not the war itself but its ripples, its side effects. But the war does take on a kind of metaphorical presence in the "Time Passes" section of Virginia Woolf's *To the Lighthouse*. Though war remains in the distance, it is coming closer, and though the house crumbles only figuratively, the thud of bombs reminds us that the war zone is spreading. In fact, as James M. Haule demonstrates in his study of Woolf's revisions of "Time Passes,"[4] the war comes even closer to Mrs. Ramsay's house in Woolf's earlier versions of this section of the novel, but as she reworked it, she systematically deleted the threat of war and its erosion of domestic life. In the original holograph draft, Woolf's references to the Great War are numerous and overt. The gusts of wind invading the house, which by the final version merely give off "an aimless gust of lamentation,"[5] in the holograph draft are likened to spies dispatched by the army to "bring news of the enemies dispositions, where to attack they gathered in the middle of the house, & gave together one of those aimless gusts of lamentation."[6] Mrs. MacNab, who in the published text is a witless old woman preoccupied with drink, gossip, and the creaking of her knees, is in the original draft a female embodiment of "the dumb persistency of the fountain of life" (*OHD* 164) and of the spirit of forgiveness and tolerance:

> How Mrs. MacNab, of all people, had come to tolerate & forgive, who shall say—Mrs. MacNab, the [sic] whose existence was ignored who was nothing but a mat for kings & kaisers to tread on, who would indeed stand patiently in the streets *to see the kings go riding by,* & whose sugar and tea were now . . . reduced at their command, passes . . . understanding. (*OHD* 164–65)

Finally, the caretaker's son, who ultimately becomes simply "a great one for work—one of those quiet ones" (*TTL* 212), originally goes about his job of mowing the lawn like a war machine: "even now he would waste no words with the women in the window, only grinned & spat, & resumed again that rhythmic singsong stroke, which . . . advanced like the sweep of an invincible army over the . . . insurgents rioting & wary in the tumult up the bank & over the lawn & . . . laid them flat" (*OHD* 183). In a novel that passionately desires creative interplay between male and female habits of mind and culture, perhaps Woolf could not bear to listen to what her pen was telling her about men and women and war. Certainly, she creates for publication a far more soothing version of the relation between the sexes than she entertains in the privacy of her first draft.

The Great War, other women novelists of the postwar era more openly insist, lends a particular urgency to the struggle between the sexes. "In the light of the shell-fire," they find it difficult to sustain the illusions they cherished about men, their rulers, and their protectors. In *After Leaving Mr. Mackenzie*, a novel set in Paris in the late twenties, Jean Rhys rarely mentions the war, but the relations she depicts between women and men are starkly lit by its shell-fire. Romance is dead in Julia Martin's Paris. The novel's heroine set out from London right after the armistice to begin her "career of chance," but by the time the novel opens ten years later, she is down and out in Paris. The war that men had waged overtly against each other, they now wage covertly against women: "When [Julia] thought of the combination of Mr. Mackenzie and Maitre Legros, all sense of reality deserted her and it seemed to her that there were no limits at all to their joint power of defeating and hurting her."[7] While one of Julia's lovers says the war taught him to believe in bad luck and another says the war taught him something about cracking up, Julia's lessons about bad luck and cracking up begin when the war ends. Julia "rather liked the air raids" (*ALM* 152), the war was for her "a funny time. A mad reckless time" (*ALM* 68), and its harsh realities come home to her only when organized society turns its attention back home: "Together, the two [Mackenzie and Legros] perfectly represented organized society, in which she had no place and against which she had not a dog's chance" (*ALM* 22). "It was the hour between dog and wolf, as they say" (*ALM* 191), the novel concludes, recalling the pattern on the wallpaper of the first of many cheap hotels in which Julia Martin finds refuge: "A large bird, sitting on the branch of a tree, faced, with open beak, a strange, mindless creature, half-bird, half-lizard, which also had its beak open and its neck stretched in a belligerent attitude" (*ALM* 10). Jean Rhys could not have known she was writing between the wars, yet her novels are drenched with the despair, loathing, and indignation of a woman crushed in the machinery of a bellicose patriarchal civilization.

Rhys, like most women novelists before her, is not as interested in the experience of war as she is in what sort of faith and confidence women can have in men who make wars. With World War II, the Cold War, and the arms race, war invades the lives and consciousness of American and European women. Women are still banned from combat, but the war zone is everywhere and women are no longer protected from its direct effects. In World War II, millions upon millions of civilians are gassed, shot, starved, bombed indiscriminately. The Cold War gives birth to a stockpile of arms sufficient to annihilate the human race many times over. Doris Lessing, in *The Golden Notebook*, records Anna Wulf's passionate resistance to acknowledging that war is a possible, a permissible, indeed a very popular masculine activity, but Anna does finally admit to her consciousness what she calls the experience of war:

> I was invaded by terror, the terror of nightmares, I was experiencing the fear of war as one does in nightmares, not the intellectual balancing of probabilities, possibilities, but knowing, with my nerves and imagination, the fear of war. What I was reading in the newspapers strewn all round me became real, not an abstract intellectual fear. There was a kind of shifting of the balances of my brain, of the way I had been thinking, the same kind of realignment as when, a few days before, words like democracy, liberty, freedom, had faded under pressure of a new sort of understanding of the real movement of the world towards dark, hardening power. I *knew*, but of course the word, written, cannot convey the quality of this knowing, that whatever already is has its logic and its force, that the great armouries

of the world have their inner force, and that my terror, the real nerve-terror of the nightmare, was part of the force. I felt this, like a vision, in a new kind of knowing.[8]

A shifting of the balances of the brain is required for Anna to invest war with any kind of actuality and to admit that her own consciousness reflects the movement of the world toward dark, hardening power.

Like most women novelists, Joan Didion has been inclined to avoid any wars she can walk around. Her early thoughts about Vietnam are located in Haight-Ashbury. "Slouching Towards Bethlehem" records not the war in Asia but the culture that war spawned at home. World War II fills her mind in the intense silence of the "19,000 graves in the vast sunken crater above Honolulu."[9] Her first two novels feature neurotic, well-heeled West Coast women whose brushes with the nuclear peril or the wars around the world are rare, accidental, and unexamined. In the last decade, however, in a voyage that began with *A Book of Common Prayer* and ended with *Salvador*, Didion has forced herself to stand where a war is going on.

"You have to pick the places you don't walk away from,"[10] Leonard Douglas tells his wife, Charlotte, in *A Book of Common Prayer* when she informs him of her decision to remain in Boca Grande, a thinly disguised portrait of El Salvador in the mid-seventies. The necessity that draws Didion to any war zone is perhaps more urgent and interesting than the necessity that dictates her particular choice of Central America; still, El Salvador is not the choice of most contemporary American novelists. Descended from members of the party that chose not to attempt a crossing of the Sierras in winter, and born and raised in the center of California's Central Valley, Joan Didion has a map of the world that does not correspond to those of East Coast and European intellectuals. Haunted by World War II, she does not look toward Europe or Russia. She looks west at Hawaii and the Pacific. Didion is drawn toward Central America by the same map of the world that makes Hawaii the appropriate place for thinking about World War II. The war zones in Central America are, for her, the ones closest to home. If her family history, her place of birth, her respect for heat do not fully account for her interest in El Salvador, the kind of war being fought there may. The "unpleasantness" in El Salvador does not immediately threaten nuclear extinction or global conflict. It is a small war in a small country, a war that is overlooked because it never stops, a war that engages the attention of the Super Powers only sporadically and usually unofficially. More crucially, it is a war being waged by identifiable men: husbands, fathers, brothers, lovers, the men sitting at the next table at the Escalon Sheraton. Grace Strasser-Mendana, the narrator of A *Book of Common Prayer*, succinctly sums up war in Boca Grande when she says:

> There you had it. The *guerrilleros* would stage their "expropriations" and leave their communiques about the "People's Revolution" and everyone would know who was financing the *guerrilleros* but for a while no one would know for whose benefit the *guerrilleros* were being financed. In the end the *guerrilleros* would all be shot and the true players would be revealed.
> *Mirabile dictu.*
> People we know. (*BCP* 211)

Didion's insistence, in both A *Book of Common Prayer* and *Salvador,* that men we know are making the wars around us, is a measure of how close, for her, war has come to home. Like Rhys, she cannot disentangle men at war from men in bed. In A *Book of Common Prayer*, Boca Grande is the historical correlative of the war zone the American home has become, and sexual relations between men and women in America mirror the internecine warfare waged so incessantly by the Strasser-Mendana brothers in Boca Grande. When Grace Strasser-Mendana tells Charlotte Douglas "about a village on the Orinoco where female children were ritually scarred on the inner thigh by their first sexual partners, the point being to scar the female with the male's totem," Charlotte sees nothing extraordinary in this. "I mean, that's pretty much what happens everywhere, isn't it," she responds. "Somebody cuts you? Where it doesn't show?" (*BCP* 85).

Before going to El Salvador to report on the war there, Joan

Didion imaginatively approached the alien terrain through the consciousness of Charlotte Douglas and of Grace Strasser-Mendana. Charlotte Douglas bears a striking resemblance to the heroines of Didion's first two novels, Maria of *Play It As It Lays* and Lily of *Run River*. All three are WASP, western American women, "unstable," sexually compelling and compulsive, enmeshed in a web of violence spun by men they know, and prone to tailoring the facts to their most consoling interpretation. What distinguishes Charlotte from Maria and Lily is the extent to which war has invaded her home. Her second husband, Leonard, is a left-wing lawyer who is "making the revolution in Bohemian Grove" (*BCP* 75). He runs guns to South America and the Middle East, and boasts a 10′ by 16′ Warhol silk screen of Mao, courtesy of the Alameda Three, "or maybe it had been one of the Tacoma Eleven or some Indian or Panther or heir to a motion-picture studio, Charlotte could never keep Leonard's clients straight" (*BCP* 62). Charlotte's daughter, Marin, has just hijacked an L1011 and gone underground with an organization Marin describes as revolutionary in character because "all our activity is defined as revolutionary" (*BCP* 82). Charlotte's first husband, Warren Bogart, is waging a private war against women and the family: he breaks up homes and marriages, beats up women. Charlotte enters an even more intimate relation with war in her status as *la norteamericana*, representative of American womanhood in Boca Grande. In *la norteamericana* (*la norteamericana* cunt, to Antonio Strasser-Mendana), war at home and war abroad intersect; Charlotte is the common target of sexual and international masculine enmities.

Perhaps because war is closing in on her, Charlotte outdoes Maria and Lily in the intensity of her commitment to self-delusion. Romance is not dead in Charlotte Douglas. Though it may die with her at the end of the novel, Charlotte herself remains "hopeful," energetically committed to finding in the facts an interpretation helpful to the human community:

That Episcopal day school Marin attended from the age of four until she entered Berkeley had as its aim "the development of a realistic but optimistic attitude," and it was characteristic of Charlotte that whenever the phrase "realistic but optimistic" appeared in a school communique she read it as "realistic and optimistic." (BCP 68)

When the facts are recalcitrant, Charlotte dwells in potentiality: a film festival could turn Boca Grande around overnight, a boutique could "pick up the character of the entire neighborhood" (BCP 218). When Grace encounters in one of Charlotte's "Letters from Boca Grande" a description of the country as "the economic fulcrum of the Americas," Grace points out that, while "planes between say, Los Angeles and Bogota, or New York and Quito, sometimes stopped in Boca Grande to refuel and paid an inflated landing fee" and "passengers on such flights often left a dollar or two in the airport slot machines during the time required for refueling," this does not "constitute, in the classical sense an economic fulcrum."

> What I was overlooking entirely, Charlotte said, was what Boca Grande "could become."
> A "Letter" from a city or a country, I suggested, was conventionally understood to be a factual report on the city or country, not as it "could become" but as it "was."
> Not necessarily, Charlotte said. (BCP 15)

Charlotte assumes the rest of the human race shares her concern for human suffering and her aspirations for a better world. When, during a cholera epidemic in Boca Grande, the vaccine Charlotte is dispensing is stolen at gun point by one of Antonio's henchmen, Charlotte's confidence flags, but she readily accepts the explanation that the army, with its greater resources, has taken over her humanitarian work. Charlotte rarely cries in this novel, but she does the evening she tells at dinner what happened at Progreso one afternoon some months later. Antonio gave Carmen an M-16, Charlotte says, and let her shoot up the place: "They were only shooting the crates. . . . Unopened crates of Lederle vaccine. . . . Cholera. It ran on the street when they shot up the crates" (BCP 238–39).

When her fellow men behave in ways Charlotte cannot take a hopeful view of, she retreats to a fiction of family loyalty. People are beasts who kill one another for sport, but blood stands by blood, parents and children care for each other, family dies with family. The lie to Charlotte's fiction of the family is, of course, her "unamusing" view of the relation that generates the family, but Charlotte resolves this contradiction by refusing to acknowledge the sexual relation as a real connection, unless blood mingles in a child. Charlotte "forgets" she slept with Pete Wright after he told her her father died alone and in pain. Charlotte is convinced she has nothing to fear from a revolution in Boca Grande because she is not connected with Gerardo "really," she is not connected with Victor "actually." Warren's claim on her is through Marin, and Carlota's death signals the dissolution of Charlotte's connection with Leonard. Like Grace's aunt in Denver, Charlotte "locates the marriage bed as the true tropic of fever and disquiet" (BCP 84).

Though the marriage bed is Charlotte's war zone, her protected zone is family, kin. She is tormented by her failures as a daughter and sister. Her brother Dicky and his wife and children are strangers to her. She wasn't there when her father died, she wasn't there when her mother died, she won't be there when the father of her child dies. Charlotte's consciousness of her own betrayals leads her finally to limit the relations in which loyalty is to be expected to her relations with her daughters. So intent is she on salvaging a hopeful view of this relation that she will not let her incurably ill, newborn baby girl die without her. At the end of the novel, Charlotte says she has walked away from places all her life, but she does not walk away from the horror of watching this infant die:

> The baby did not die at the Merida airport but an hour later, in the parking lot of the Coca-Cola bottling plant on the road back into town. The baby had gone into convulsions and projectile vomiting in the taxi and Charlotte had made the driver stop in the parking lot. She walked with the baby on the dark asphalt. She sang to the baby out on the edge of the asphalt where the rushes grew and a few trailers were parked. By the time the baby died the taxi had left but it was only a mile or two to the Centro Medico de Yucatan and Charlotte walked there with the baby in her arms, trusting at last, its

vomit spent. The doctor did not speak English but marked the death
certificate in English: *Death by complications.* (BCP 150–51)

Charlotte spends even more physical, moral, and imaginative
energy on salvaging her relation with her daughter Marin. "Marin's trip to Utah," is how Charlotte refers to the hijacking of the
L1011. "Marin and I are inseparable" is Charlotte's constant
refrain, even when she is in Boca Grande and Marin's where-
abouts are unknown. For Grace, Charlotte spins a fantasy of
mother and daughter worthy of the pages of the only two things
Charlotte had read before she met Warren, *Vogue* and Charlotte
Brontë. The absence of Banyan trees at the American embassy
reminds Charlotte of the day she and Marin played hide-and-
seek among the thousand trunks of the Great Banyan at the
Calcutta Botanical Garden: "It had been 'the most lyrical' day.
She and Marin had 'devoured' coconut ice for lunch. She and
Marin had wandered beneath the Great Banyan at noon and
stayed until after dark" (BCP 35). The presence of colored lights
strung outside the Capilla del Mar, a souvenir of "the season
when a deranged Haitian dentist convinced the Minister of
Health to string the entire city of Boca Grande with a web of
colored lights as a specific against typhoid" (BCP 47), reminds
Charlotte of the Tivoli Gardens, "where she had once flown with
Marin for the weekend. Her face came alive with pleasure as she
described this adult's dream of a weekend a child might like,
described the puppet shows, the watermills, the picnic with the
child" (BCP 47). Some weeks later Charlotte says that actually
Marin ran a fever the whole weekend and they never left the
hotel.

Charlotte is able to deny, revise, or forget even the most recalcitrant facts about Marin's revolutionary activities—her ditching
of the harelip, her use of Charlotte's grandmother's gold pin in
the timing mechanism of the bomb—in order to sustain her
consoling fiction of their relationship. She goes to the airport
every day in Boca Grande to meet the plane Marin will arrive on
to join her mother: "In a certain dim way Charlotte believed that
she had located herself at the very cervix of the world, the place

through which a child lost to history must eventually pass" (*BCP* 197). But when Leonard arrives in Boca Grande bearing two brutal facts—Marin did not want to go to her father's funeral, and Marin does not want to come to her mother—Charlotte's resistance cracks. "So in the first place it's not even Marin," Charlotte makes a last desperate effort at an explanation of the facts which accords with her desire, "Marin would have found Warren. Marin would have found me" (*BCP* 253). But her last words to Leonard about her daughter acknowledge that loyalty, even between mother and daughter, exists only in Charlotte's mind: "I don't have to see Marin because I have Marin in my mind and Marin has me in her mind" (*BCP* 257).

The Charlotte Marin has in mind suggests the mutual propensity of mother and daughter to romanticize when confronted with war. While Charlotte is willing to accept that the protected zone has dwindled from home to mother and daughter, when that zone is invaded, she gets herself shot. War is everywhere, she concludes, so there's nowhere to walk to. Marin, a daughter of history as well as of Charlotte, fabricates from the pervasiveness of war a consoling fiction of her own. War mercifully dissolves her obligations to family and, most particularly, to her mother. "We ask no one's permission to make the revolution," Marin says on the tape released after the hijacking, and she tells Grace she remembers her mother only in a tennis dress. When Grace admits she didn't understand Charlotte, Marin snaps, "Try a class analysis" (*BCP* 259). When Grace mentions that Charlotte worked in a birth control clinic in Boca Grande, Marin retorts, "Classic. . . . Absolutely classic. . . . Birth control is *the* most flagrant example of how the ruling class practices genocide" (*BCP* 213). That Charlotte is the enemy in her daughter's war is recognized finally even by Charlotte when, just before her death, she mails to her daughter the "memento from the man who financed the Tupamaros," the emerald ring which Grace's husband gave Leonard for guns and which Leonard gave Charlotte for love.

Though Charlotte and her daughter resist certain facts about war with equal passion, Grace, the narrator of *A Book of Com-*

*mon Prayer*, offers a consciousness apparently quite pervious to fact. She is dying of cancer, an amateur student of biochemistry, a witness for years of behavior among her father, in-laws, and son, which leaves her little space for hopeful interpretation. At Christmas, she can coolly watch Antonio amusing himself by shooting up the creche. She knows brother plots against brother, and son against father; she knows when one brother is about to oust another; she knows exactly when to get out. Grace's clear-eyed though paralyzing cynicism is a tempting alternative to Charlotte's frenetic self-delusion, but Grace herself learns late in the novel that she has harbored a consoling fiction of her own. Grace cherishes the belief that her deceased husband, alone among the Strasser-Mendanas, did not make war and did not kill his brothers, until Leonard informs her that the man who financed the Tupamaros and gave him the emerald was her husband. "I am more like Charlotte than I thought I was" (*BCP* 268), Grace is forced to conclude at the close of the novel.

Through Charlotte, Didion purges her reluctance to face the facts about men and war but, like Grace, Didion sustains certain consoling illusions of her own in *A Book of Common Prayer*. We may argue whether Charlotte's death commands respect or regret, but there is no question that it commands attention. Charlotte is the only war victim we mourn in this novel, hers is the only death that counts. The first page announces her fate ("She died hopeful"), and the final pages tell of the body tossed on the American embassy lawn. As the novel witnesses this single fatality, so Didion in the novel witnesses not the war in El Salvador but the deadly encounter between that war and the historically protected, determinedly optimistic *norteamericana*. We hear of other deaths: in the normal process by which government changes hands in Boca Grande, hundreds die when the *guerrilleros* are sold out; when Antonio hijacks the Lederle vaccine, cholera kills hundreds, most of them children; when a bomb explodes in the birth control clinic, four die. But what we remember about the bomb in the clinic is that Charlotte bled "all over the place" because she had her period. What we remember about the cholera epidemic is that Charlotte cried. What we

remember about the slaughter of hundreds of civilians and soldiers in the revolution in Boca Grande is the slaughter of one
American woman, caught in the crossfire.

In *A Book of Common Prayer,* Didion maintains a protected
zone between herself and war, between women and war. What
Charlotte says wrongly of Gerardo, she says truly of war, she is
not connected "really." But Charlotte is intimately connected
with men who make wars. "*Norteamericana* cunt" is a point not
lost on Grace, who repeatedly describes Charlotte as laden with
"sexual freight," as though war has dissolved for men the obligation to regard Charlotte as anything other than an answer to
appetite (Boca Grande, big mouth, "the cervix of the world").
Charlotte says she is not connected with her lovers "really," as
though war relieves her of any obligation to regard men as
anything other than mouths to be fed. War is a man's game in *A
Book of Common Prayer,* and Charlotte steadfastly refuses to pay
any attention to it, as if disassociation remains possible. She
draws a sharp line between herself and war, she is "*de afeura,*" an
outsider to this territory, and so is Grace, and so, finally, is
Didion. She is not witnessing war in Boca Grande, she is witnessing the faces of men and women in the light of the shell-fire.

Joan Didion did not intend *A Book of Common Prayer* to be
her letter from El Salvador. Boca Grande is part of the landscape
of Charlotte Douglas's story, it functions as metaphor, symbol,
and reflection of Charlotte's experience. The novel gives us El
Salvador not as it "is" but as it clarifies the life and death of *la
norteamericana. Salvador,* however, is Didion's letter (her "grim-
gram" even) from El Salvador in the conventional sense, a
factual report on the country as it is. It is not common for
novelists to follow a fictitious account of a place with a factual
report, but in Didion's case the process seems natural, even
inevitable. Her experience of war has been literary and imagi-
nary, her inclination has been to improve upon accounts because, as she says of El Salvador, "the unimproved situation . . .
was such that to consider it was to consider moral extinction."[11]
To get at the facts, *la verdad,* Didion has to penetrate both the
fictions about El Salvador and her own desire to disassociate, to

fictionalize. With *Salvador*, Didion completes the passage she began in *A Book of Common Prayer*; she crosses the line between *la norteamericana* and war to report from inside the war zone, from a place "bad, terrible, squalid beyond anyone's power to understand it without experiencing it" (*S*, 88), from a place where "the dead and pieces of the dead turn up . . . everywhere, everyday" (*S* 19).

From El Salvador, Didion writes, "Disassociation is more difficult here. The disfigurement is too routine. The locations are too near, the dates too recent" (*S* 17). Perhaps Didion lacks Doris Lessing's confidence in the imagination; certainly she has been unwilling to accept any mental or spiritual substitute (any nightmare or hallucination) for the actual experience of the terror of war. Her exploration of El Salvador, as the opening quotation from *Heart of Darkness* suggests, has its literary analogue in Conrad's exploration of the Congo, but the dissimilarities between the two works are finally more interesting than the similarities. As Conrad approaches a full recognition of the horrors of which the human race and, more disturbingly for Conrad, the white man ("one of us," as he puts it) are capable, his vision dims, a language of abstraction replaces concrete detail. Horror, students of writing are often advised, is best rendered by this sort of linguistic vagueness, by a general invitation to the reader to supply his or her own darkest fantasies. Detail consoles, even trivializes, by limiting horror to a specific time and place. Perhaps because Didion, as a woman, does not identify with the horrors she beholds in El Salvador, her vision only sharpens, grows more relentlessly concrete in the face of the unspeakable. In Conrad the horror is dark and obscure; in Didion it is appallingly manifest, a "particular darkness." The effect of *Salvador* is not of a descent into dream but of a harsh awakening, and Didion clings to detail as though it alone convinces her she is in the presence of the actual.

For the reader who comes to *Salvador* from *A Book of Common Prayer*, the effect of an awakening not from but into terror, of a shocking encounter with the actual in the apparently fictitious, is intensified by the repeated discovery that the fictions of Boca

Grande are the facts, even the facts "improved," of El Salvador. Those colored lights that remind Charlotte of her blissful weekend with Marin at the Tivoli Gardens are not, in fact, the inspiration of either Joan Didion or a deranged Haitian dentist. They are the inspiration of General Maximiliano Hernandes Martinez, dictator of El Salvador from 1931 to 1944. According to the United States Government Printing Office's *Area Handbook for El Salvador,* Martinez "kept bottles of colored water that he dispensed as cures for almost any disease, including cancer and heart trouble, and relied on complex magical formulas for the solution of national problems. . . . During an epidemic of smallpox in the capital, he attempted to halt its spread by stringing the city with a web of colored lights" (*S* 54). El Progreso is not the literary invention of Joan Didion, not a visionary landscape of a waste of shame, but the actual product of a

> central hallucination of the Molina and Romero regimes, the projected beach resorts, the Hyatt, the Pacific Paradise, tennis, golf, waterskiing, condos, Costa del Sol; the visionary invention of a tourist industry in yet another republic where the leading cause of death is gastrointestinal infection. In the general absence of tourists these hotels have since been abandoned, ghost resorts on the empty Pacific beaches. (*S* 13)

Charlotte's boutique and film festival suddenly seem plausible, even realistic, when juxtaposed with delusions on this scale.

*Salvador* strips away the fictions that insulate women from war and the reader of *A Book of Common Prayer* from the realities of El Salvador. Romance is dead in El Salvador. The photo albums with "plastic covers bearing soft-focus color photographs of young Americans in dating situations (strolling through autumn foliage on one album, recumbent in a field of daisies on another)" (*S* 18) house not wedding pictures but forensic photographs.

> The bodies . . . are often broken into unnatural positions, and the faces to which the bodies are attached (when they are attached) are equally unnatural, sometimes unrecognizable as human faces, obliterated by acid or beaten to a mash of misplaced ears and teeth or slashed ear to ear and invaded by insects. (*S* 16–17)

The women of El Salvador wait for hours every day to pour over these color photos, looking for husbands, brothers, sisters, children who have disappeared. The landscape, too, houses horrors beneath soft-focus covers. Puerta del Diablo is "still described, in the April-July issue of *Aboard TACA*," the magazine provided passengers on the national airline of El Salvador, as "offering excellent subjects for color photography."

> Puerta del Diablo is a "view site" in an older and distinctly literary tradition, nature as lesson, an immense cleft rock through which half of El Salvador seems framed, a site so romantic and "mystical," so theatrically sacrificial in aspect, that it might be a cosmic parody of nineteenth-century landscape painting. The place presents itself as pathetic fallacy: the sky "broods," the stones "weep," a constant seepage of water weighting the ferns and moss. The foliage is thick and slick with moisture. The only sound is a steady buzz, I believe of cicadas. (S 19–20)

Unless an execution is occurring at the top, it is necessary to go down to see the bodies: "The way down is hard. Slabs of stone, slippery with moss, are set into the vertiginous cliff, and it is down this cliff that one begins the descent to the bodies, or what is left of the bodies, pecked and maggoty masses of flesh, bone, hair" (S 21). "Nothing fresh today, I hear," an American embassy official remarks, when Didion says she has just returned from Puerta del Diablo. "Were there any on top?" another wants to know (S 20).

The terror of encountering "the dead and pieces of the dead" in every landscape, in every "excellent subject for color photography," is accompanied in El Salvador by the terror of encountering one's own death in every landscape and every occasion. After her visit to Puerta del Diablo, Didion finds herself asking definite questions about the man and three small children who were playing on top while a woman started and stopped a Toyota pickup. A Toyota pick-up, a Cherokee Chief sighted anywhere, but especially in the vicinity of the Sheraton or any popular execution site or body dump, incite a certain tremor, so commonly are they associated with death and disappearance. Sitting with her

husband alone one evening on the canopied porch of a restaurant near the Mexican embassy, Didion is "demoralized, undone, humiliated by fear" of two human shadows: "One shadow
sat behind the smoked-glass windows of a Cherokee Chief parked
at the curb in front of the restaurant; the other crouched between
the pumps at the Esso station next door, carrying a rifle" (S 26).
In the "leafy stillness" of a sidewalk in the wealthy San Benito dis-
trict, where "pools of blossoms lie undisturbed," Didion opens
her bag to check an address, and hears "the clicking of metal on
metal all up and down the street" (S 22).

In one of her letters from Boca Grande, Charlotte writes,
" 'The outlook is not all bright. . . . Nor is the outlook all black.'
Paragraph. 'Nonetheless—.' " There she is blocked. Grace points
out, "If you say 'the outlook is not all bright' and then you say 'nor
is the outlook all black,' then you can't start the next sentence
with 'nevertheless.' It can't possibly mean anything." When
Charlotte replies, "It's not just a new sentence. It's a new paragraph," it occurs to Grace that she "had never before had so
graphic an illustration of how the consciousness of the human
organism is carried in its grammar" (BPC 233–34). The consciousness of El Salvador, too, is carried in its grammar. To
disappear, in El Salvador, is more commonly a transitive than an
intransitive verb (i.e., *desconocidos*, unknown men, disappeared
him). In this instance, the grammar of the country reveals a
surprising respect for reality, perhaps because the origin of the
usage is popular rather than official. Among officials of the
country, language is appreciated not for its descriptive but for its
fictive possibilities. Under investigation, "even the most apparently straight-forward event takes on, in El Salvador, elusive
shadows, like a fragment of retrieved legend" (S 67). As Didion
pursues information pertaining to the crash of a Hughes 500-D
helicopter, even the facts she thought she had fade into fictions:
"the crash of this particular helicopter became, like everything
else in El Salvador, an occasion of rumor, doubt, suspicion,
conflicting reports, and finally a kind of listless uneasiness" (S 67–
68).

El Salvador's is not a culture, Didion writes, "in which a

high value is placed on the definite" (*S* 61). When Didion tells a Salvadoran woman at an embassy party that she hopes to tell *la verdad* about El Salvador, the woman beams, assuming Didion is using *la verdad* in the code that means *la verdad* according to Roberto D'Aubuisson. Numbers, statements of fact, *la verdad* often express things wished for, things that might be or should be rather than things that are, and to change the name of a thing is assumed to change its nature. This tendency to accord language a life of its own has its flowering, Didion suggests, in the work of Gabriel Garcia Marquez, and its corruption in the linguistic collusion between the governments of El Salvador and the United States: "Language as it is now used in El Salvador is the language of advertising, of persuasion, the product being one or another of the *soluciones* crafted in Mexico or Panama or Washington, which is part of the place's pervasive obscenity" (*S* 65).

The "big stick" the United States uses to prod the government of El Salvador with is economic aid, but the language in which the "delicate process of certification" is conducted has "a distinctly circular aspect (the aid was the card with which we got the Salvadorans to do it our way, and appearing to do it our way was the card with which the Salvadorans got the aid)" (*S* 94). Negotiations on aid occur strictly in the realm of appearances; the Salvadoran government must be made to "'appear' to do what the American government needed done in order to make it 'appear' that American aid was justified" (*S* 93). In this effort, Roberto D'Aubuisson, the "democratically elected" president of El Salvador, has made it "hard for everybody" (*S* 93). Former ambassador to El Salvador, Robert E. White, has described D'Aubuisson as a pathological killer, and even "in-country" the adjectives used to describe him do not inspire confidence. Accused of twice plotting to overthrow the government, strongly suspected of the murder of Archbishop Romero and of spearheading the most active death squad in El Salvador, D'Aubuisson, it was feared by American embassy officials, "could queer everybody's ability to refer to his election as a vote for freedom" (*S* 30). But he didn't "queer" Ronald Reagan's:

Since the Exodus from Egypt, historians have written of those who sacrificed and struggled for freedom: the stand at Thermopylae, the revolt of Spartacus, the storming of the Bastille, the Warsaw uprising in World War II. More recently we have seen evidence of the same human impulse in one of the developing nations in Central America. For months and months the world news media covered the fighting in El Salvador. Day after day, we were treated to stories and film slanted toward the brave freedom fighters battling oppressive government forces in behalf of the silent suffering people of that tortured country. Then one day those silent suffering people were offered a chance to vote to choose the kind of government they wanted. Suddenly the freedom fighters in the hills were exposed for what they really are: Cuban-backed guerrillas. . . . On election day the people of El Salvador, an unprecedented [1.5 million] of them, braved ambush and gunfire, trudging miles to vote for freedom. (S 28)

American officials in El Salvador are less inclined to place any event in that country in such company. Their language, when not strikingly reminiscent of Charlotte's, tends toward the breezy and the casual. Of D'Aubuisson, American embassy people say, "You take a guy who's young, and everything 'young' implies, you send him signals, he plays ball, then we play ball" (S 29). As the United States ambassador's sheep dog tears across the lawn at the sound of rifle practice at Escuelar Militar, the ambassador says in a Montana twang, "Only time we had any quiet up here . . . was when we sent the whole school up to Benning" (S 87).

That Didion, before going to El Salvador, had enjoyed the privilege accorded *la norteamericana* of disassociation from war is strikingly illustrated by a conversation she has with an El Salvadoran woman who works for her in Los Angeles. The woman, whose two brothers had been killed in their beds in El Salvador, vehemently cautions Didion about what she must do and not do to stay alive in that country: "We must not go out at night. We must stay off the street whenever possible. We must never ride in buses or taxis, never leave the capital, never imagine that our passports could protect us. We must not even consider the hotel a safe place: people were killed in hotels" (*S* 77). "Trying for a light touch," Didion says probably she will spend all her time in church.

> She became still more agitated, and I realized I had spoken as a *norteamericana:* churches had not been to this woman the neutral ground they had been to me. I must remember: Archbishop Romero killed saying mass in the Chapel of the Divine Providence Hospital in El Salvador. I must remember: more than thirty people killed at Archbishop Romero's funeral in the Metropolitan Cathedral in San Salvador. I must remember: more than twenty people killed before that on the steps of the Metropolitan Cathedral. CBS had filmed it. It had been on television, the bodies jerking, those alive crawling over the dead as they tried to get out of range. I must understand: the Church was dangerous. (*S* 78)

Only in El Salvador does Didion give up her neutral ground, her privilege of not witnessing war, and only in El Salvador does she take the full measure of that privilege. Walking back from the Metrocenter, billed locally as "Central America's Largest Shopping Mall," Didion experiences her own *noche obscura:* "As I waited to cross back over the Boulevard de los Heros to the Camino Real I noticed soldiers herding a young civilian into a van, their guns at the boy's back, and I walked straight ahead, not wanting to see anything at all" (*S* 36). Perhaps it is natural to look away from horrors we cannot assuage or avert, and certainly women have been encouraged to look away from the horrors of war. But Didion compels us to share her recognition that our desire not to see anything at all leads not to moral superiority but to moral extinction.

## NOTES

1. H. W. Garrod, "Jane Austen: A Depreciation," in *Discussions of Jane Austen*, ed. William Heath (Boston, 1961).
2. Virginia Woolf, *A Room of One's Own* (New York, 1957), 15.
3. Vera Brittain, *Testament of Youth* (New York, 1980), 291–92.
4. James M. Haule, "*To the Lighthouse* and the Great War: The Evidence of Virginia Woolf's Revisions of 'Times Passes.'"

5. Virginia Woolf, *To the Lighthouse* (New York, 1957), 191. Hereafter referred to as *TTL*.

6. *To the Lighthouse: The Original Holograph Draft*, ed. Susan Dick (Toronto, 1982), 156. Hereafter referred to as *OHD*.

7. Jean Rhys, *After Leaving Mr. Mackenzie* (New York, 1974), 22. Hereafter referred to as *ALM*.

8. Doris Lessing, *The Golden Notebook* (New York, 1973), 588–89.

9. Joan Didion, *Slouching Towards Bethlehem* (New York, 1979), 192. Hereafter referred to as *STB*.

10. Joan Didion, *A Book of Common Prayer* (New York, 1977), 256. Hereafter referred to as *BCP*.

11. Joan Didion, *Salvador* (New York, 1983), 92. Hereafter referred to as *S*.

# Lydia among the Uniforms

**C**arol didn't have many friends on the island that winter of '43. We'd have drinks now and then with the coast guard at the Shore Hotel, but somebody had to mind the girls and mostly she stayed behind and I went alone. I'd be dying for a break from the chatter and the runny noses and the Mommy, Mommy, Mommy all day long, and Carol would say, Go on, you're only young once, and usually I couldn't say no. Besides, Carol hated guns, and all the boys we knew in the coast guard felt naked without them. How can you have a conversation, Carol would say when a guy offered to buy her a drink, with a person with a gun? Bully boy's here, she'd shout when any man came to our door with a gun, even the ones she liked. I'd say, It's Jimbo, remember Jimbo? He dug the car out of the garage after the hurricane. I'd say, It's Ralph, you know Ralph, he's going to sit with the girls tonight so you and I can see that Hepburn movie you've been on about since it opened last week. And Carol would say, He's a bully boy just the same. You can tell by the gun. Got so the boys left their guns under the couch on the porch before they knocked on our door, though it was against regulations and the Admiral owned the house across the street.

Carol was German, too. At least her mother was. So was the wife of the Admiral across the street. So were most of the wives between 20th and 30th Streets who flocked to the shore every summer to sit on their front stoops and cluck about the filthy habits of the Italian Catholic women who were their neighbors back home. Krautsville, the coast guard called the neighborhood when Carol wasn't around.

Carol liked being German as much as she liked guns. Hun's home, she'd shout when she strolled in with the groceries and cigarettes she'd gotten Jimbo to buy her at the PX. Time you got these girls in uniform, she said the afternoon she came home with matching sunsuits for Katie and Lizzie. Lollies for the little Aryans, she said as she doled out the lollypops the girls drooled down the front of their matching sunsuits and stuck in their hair.

Carol was sharp with everybody that year, except the girls. Look, she'd say, shoving a newspaper in my face with a picture of some S.S. officer clicking his heels. Isn't he the spitting image of Austen in his uniform? Austen who? I'd say coolly. But news of the concentration camps was getting more detailed and the coast guard was broadcasting some new kind of bomb that could blow New York City off the map and Carol was keeping a scrap book of all the nastiest bits she found in the paper each day, so I was surprised when she took to Lydia the way she did.

Lydia was the ghost in the Admiral's house across the street. We first noticed the lights in late January. I thought we should call the coast guard but Carol said, No, they're too trigger happy these days. She called the Admiral's wife instead, who said the woman was her friend and we should mind our own business.

We never saw the woman on the beach or at the grocery store or the PX or the five and dime or the movies. Once we saw her coming out of the sea shell store but she didn't speak or smile or nod, she just froze in the shadow of the door until we were gone. At night she lit candles in the Admiral's den and paced the room for hours, her angular frame swinging to and fro behind the lace curtains like a pendulum in a grandfather clock. Is she still at it, I'd ask Carol when I joined her on the porch after the girls were asleep, and Carol would nod to the rhythm of the woman's walk, and I'd catch it too and we three would be hammering out the minutes until Carol or I had to say something smart. She keeps the trains running on time, I said one cold, moonlit night. Must be German, came from Carol, we Germans love a march.

Even after the night in late February when we found Lydia lurking around in our garage after some man she said she thought she saw there and I would have shot her if Carol had let me keep the gun Jimbo gave me, Lydia could have stayed the Admiral's ghost as far as I was concerned. Everybody needed somebody to make wise cracks about during the war, even Carol had herself. But Carol wouldn't let her alone after that night. She took her our coffee and butter and books, and pretty soon she was at Lydia's as much as she was at home. Every night, after the girls were asleep and I could turn in the goo-goo-ga-ga for some real talk, Carol would launch into the latest installment of Lydia says.

Her husband's in the Luftwaffe, her older son is at the eastern front, Lydia says. Maybe dead, maybe still killing. She went to a concentration camp, on a tour for the good wives of the Reich. They drank tea, Lydia says, and chatted over puff pastry still warm from the oven. Did you see any with horns, her eight-year-old son wanted to know when she got home. Any with monkey hair? That's when she knew she had to go.

Night after night, I'd sit on the porch and watch Lydia walk and listen to Lydia says. The Admiral doesn't know she's in the house, Lydia says. She and his wife were schoolgirls together in Munich during the first war. Vida helped her get out, offered her husband's house here in Shipbottom as a place to hide. What could be safer, Vida told her. The place is full of Germans and he's an Admiral. Lydia doesn't have any papers, of course. She couldn't even say good-bye to her younger son, he would have reported her to Hitler Youth. Her husband will kill her if he gets his hands on her. Why not, Lydia says. He's killed so many.

Carol wanted me to meet her but I didn't feel like befriending forlorn Nazis and I tried to walk around her the day I saw her on the beach, but the girls toddled right up to her and asked her to make them a sand castle. A wisp of a smile flickered around the corners of her mouth as she dribbled wet sand on the castle, but it faded when she looked up and said, not to me but to the ocean between her and home, If only I had had daughters.

You put your girls in uniform, too, I said. You put them in uniform and you march them around and teach them to hate Jews and to love their boots better than their mothers. Always the boots, Lydia murmured, following orders. I didn't notice the diamond until her fingernails clicked against the bucket. It was the biggest rock I'd ever seen. Oh well, I said, when the war is over, you'll be wintering on the Riviera again. Lydia stood up and looked at me hard, her forty-five years in her eyes. War is never over, she said. It just comes home.

I was glad to see her go, made some crack to myself about Krauts of a different feather when she paused to chat with the old German Jew who ran the sea shell store and sat on the bench at 27th Street every afternoon between five and six.

I don't know when Carol made it a religion to go with Lydia every morning to the sea shell shop. First she came home with sea shell necklaces for Katie and Lizzie, then with an abalone ashtray and a tacky sea shell jewelry box for me, then finally one morning I asked if she'd mind the girls while Jimbo showed me around the new radar station, and she said, no, she couldn't possibly, she had to go with Lydia to the sea shell shop. Forget the butter and sugar, I snapped, unless that old Jew has an in at the PX, but Carol just looked at me sadly so I told her to go to hell with the rest of her Krauts.

The next three days we didn't speak. Carol wouldn't lift a finger for the girls, she spent her days at Lydia's, her nights locked in her room. By the fourth morning, I was crying in fury trying to get breakfast down the girls when Carol piped up behind me, I'll do the bananas if you'll go with Lydia to the shop this morning.

The walk to the Jew's was long enough to make me feel Lydia's silence. I couldn't keep my eyes off the diamond on her finger and the two shells she held like robin's eggs in the palm of her hand. Finally I said, What are the shells for? I bring two each day, Lydia held out the shells, one for each son.

None for your husband? I said, and I clicked my heels and flicked her a Nazi salute. Lydia tapped a shell with her finger-nail and said, I tell your sister-in-law, that Dorothy is hard in the head. This encounter, this excursion, it will do no good, but she insists, your Carol. She says we women must stick to-gether, especially now, especially us. Lydia clicked her heels and returned my salute, then marched briskly up the shell lined path to the sea shell shop. I was blind when I stepped in-side. A raw voice cackled, Cash on the line, Cash on the line. A flickering orange glow cast by a revolving crab shell lamp played eerily across Lydia's face and when she touched me, I jumped. Then I saw the parrot and, from the deep shadows be-hind it, a voice muttered, Hush, Lazarus.

Carol made her come, Lydia said, and the old man stepped from the shadows to hug her like a father. Never mind, he said. You go now. She handed him the shells and kissed him on each cheek. She was dark in the doorway against the bright light. Nothing to lose, Nothing to lose, the parrot crowed and then she was gone.

Just like me, my Lazarus is becoming, the old man chuckled as he disappeared behind a curtain in the back of the store, but his voice went on. I see your girls on the beach. One, she is blonde like a duckling, the other, she has curls like Shirley Temple. I see Shirley Temple at the Bijou, I see you and Carol there, too, but never Lydia. I see Shirley Temple but the rat-ta-tat-tat of her dancing shoes is a machine gun in my head and I have to leave. The old man reappeared to place a sea shell lamp carefully on the counter between us. I have trouble with Lydia, too, in the beginning. He patted my hand like I was the one with trouble now. Lydia, she sail in here tall and blonde like Queen Christina, and she hand me two shells and she say in her Nazi German, I should like these in the base of the lamp you will make me, *bitte*. Lamps I got plenty of, I say in the German this war teaches me. Sea shell, star fish, sea horse, lobster, you name it, I got it, right here in the shop, ready made. I ain't no tailor and I ain't no banker. Ready made's my first name, Cash on the line's my last. Cash on the line, Cash on the line, my Lazarus say right back, just like I teach him.

The old man stooped behind the counter and the lamp went on. Its shade was cupped like a tulip and each of its four petals was translucent as a baby's skin. In one, finely etched black arcs formed a rose, in another silken brown lines waved like wheat in a summer breeze. Pretty, no? he said from the darkness outside the halo of light. Lydia, she come back here the next day with her two shells and she say, Your children are dead but mine are still killing, and then I see how things are and I say, yes, you will bring me your shells every day so as not to forget what your children are doing and I will make you a lamp. He stepped then into the circle of light and I saw he was not much older than I was and I fled.

Jimbo was drinking his lunch at the Shore Hotel when I sat down next to him and ordered a scotch. What's the word on that Fraulein in the Admiral's house, he wanted to know. I hear she's a spy. I hear she's got binoculars and makes signals with a mirror and works some kind of shell code through the old German Jew.

Everybody's got binoculars these days, I said. And the Jew isn't old and there isn't any code. He's making her a lamp. I could have left it at that, but there was a war on and I was in it more than I knew so I said, And it isn't a mirror, it's a diamond and it's bigger than any rock you'll ever see.

Jimbo couldn't get that diamond out of his head. He made inquiries among some higher-ups in the coast guard. They were not anxious to tamper with the Admiral's guest, but Jimbo egged them on until they agreed to make a routine check of the woman's papers.

I had a feeling that morning when we passed the Admiral's house on our way to the beach to look for signs of the enemy, that the house was too still, too empty. When we came back from the beach an hour later, the ambulance was pulling away.

Lydia had told Carol more than once that she'd not go back with a drop of blood in her veins.

That night, when everybody was asleep, I tiptoed into the girls' room and cut a lock of hair from each of their heads. I dug out the sea shell jewelry box from the back of my bottom drawer and on the blue velvet cushion inside I coiled a thick blond curl of Katie's hair. Next to it I placed a lock of Lizzie's baby hair, bright as a comet against the dark blue. In the dead of night I left the box on the doorstep of the sea shell shop. The next morning the box and the lamp and the Jew were gone. Only the parrot was there to greet Jimbo and the boys when they burst through the door at dawn. Jimbo took the parrot and renamed him Jappo and taught him to say, Bombs away.

Weeks later the photograph came, though it was postmarked Shipbottom the day before Lydia died. Lydia sits in the center in a straight-backed chair, the fur of her collar prickling her chin. Behind her stands a man in a Nazi uniform laden with medals and ribbons and stripes. To her right a young man kneels in the plainer uniform of a foot soldier. A boy in the starched shorts, shirt, and tie of the Hitler Youth nestles close to her other side. Lydia is effaced by this commanding assertion of a common cause in all who surround her, but a wisp of hair escapes the artillery of hair pins aimed at keeping it in.

I offered the photograph to Carol, though it was addressed to me. No, Carol said, you've earned it. And I have, I guess, through the years. Carol's never been a real friend to me since the war and Austen and I didn't survive those years either, though we stayed married a decade longer than we should have for the sake of the girls. But Katie loves her boots now better than her mother and Lizzie says she'll never have a child. What if it's a boy, she says. What about the bomb?

I keep the photograph by my bed. It's a thin, lonely bed now and sometimes Lydia gets lost behind the pictures of Katie's boys in their scout uniforms and school uniforms and football uniforms but I always find her again and hear again on her lips the words which are never far from my own, war is never over, it just comes home.

# Reconstructing Vietnam:

## Joan Didion and Doris Lessing

One of Anna Wulf's many literary diversions, in Doris Lessing's *Golden Notebook*, is parodying herself, her work, and the culture business in general. When the Blue Bird Series of Television One-Hour Plays wants to turn Anna's first novel about war and the color bar into a "simple love story," Anna toys with the idea, constructing an opening scene drenched in a meretricious nostalgia for the emotional intensities of wartime. Anna takes a certain sour pleasure in inventing such counterfeits of her work and herself and watching them sell. In response to the editor of a literary journal who has been plaguing Anna for years for "something of yours—at last,"[1] Anna Wulf invents the journal of "a lady author of early-middle age, who [has] spent some years in an African colony and [is] afflicted with sensibility" (*TGN* 437). This lady author afflicted with sensibility discovers "the essential tragedy of the colonial situation" (*TGN* 438) in a story she records and comments upon in her journal:

> A young white farmer . . . notice[s] a young African girl of rare beauty and intelligence. He tries to influence her to educate herself, to raise herself, for her family are nothing but crude Reserve Natives. But she misunderstands his motives and falls in love. Then, when he (oh, so gently) explains his real interest in her, she turns virago and calls him ugly names. Taunts him. He, patient, bears it. But she goes to the police and tells them he has tried to rape her. He suffers the social obloquy in silence. He goes to prison accusing her only with his eyes, while she turns away in shame. It could be real, strong

> drama! It symbolizes . . . the superior spiritual status of the white man trapped by history, dragged down into the animal mud of Africa. So true, so penetrating, so *new*. (*TGN* 439)

Though Anna thinks this is all a bit thick, the editor accepts the journal entry enthusiastically, but, as Anna puts it, "my rare sensibility overcame me at the last moment and I decided to keep my privacy. Rupert sent me a note saying that he so understood, some experiences were too personal for print" (*TGN* 439).

When I think about the impact of Vietnam on literature, I think first of the soldiers' stories. Like every war, Vietnam has been remembered, and some of its memoirs, both in fiction and in fact, offer powerful and precise accounts of the experience of some of the young American men who fought there (*Going after Cacciato*, for example, or *Dispatches*). We have also had some fine coming-home novels (*In Country*, for example, and, more recently, *Paco's Story*). And we will, no doubt, if we don't already, have some fine going-back novels. That I think, instinctively, of this body of literature as *the* literature of Vietnam, is perhaps a response as much to the films as to the literature of the war. The story of the American soldier in Vietnam has proved to have a viselike grip on the imagination of Hollywood and, like the Ancient Mariner, Hollywood has to tell it again and again, and never more often than in the last few years: *Rambo, Gardens of Stone, Full Metal Jacket, Missing in Action, I, II, and III, Good Morning Vietnam, Platoon, Born on the Fourth of July*, the list goes on and on. What our films and literature of Vietnam have operated together to do in the more than twenty years since Tet is to lay down the line of the story of Vietnam, and that line is, I think, essentially the discovery of the tragedy of the colonial, or perhaps more accurately the imperial, situation in the tragedy of the white American man. With the partial exception of *The Killing Fields*, virtually all our well-known representations of Vietnam in literature and in film ask us, first and foremost, to pity the white American soldier—to share his guilt, to weigh his wounds, to forgive his degradation, to understand his loyalties, to admire his endurance, to appreciate his betrayal, to recognize the "superior spiritual status" of the American soldier "trapped by history, dragged down into the animal mud" of Vietnam. That American soldiers suffered intolerably in Vietnam is beyond question. That the character of the American soldier, indeed the character of America itself, was, as Larry Heinemann puts it in an interview with the *San Francisco Chronicle*, "squandered in Vietnam"[2] is equally beyond question. "There was this sense of *carte blanche,*" Heinemann says in the same interview. "You could do anything, stand naked in the street and piss if you wanted; there was the broadest possible permission. If you killed the wrong person, that's too bad. That was a body count. So we got brutal and mean, and the evil of it was, we really began to like it." What is not beyond question, however, is the priority we have given to American suffering and American brutalization in a war that America inflicted, for no good reason, on the entire populations of three unoffending countries on the other side of the world.

The impact of this widespread pressure to "reheroicize" the Vietnam soldier was brought home to me by an article by Bob Baker in the February 22, 1988, *Los Angeles Times* called "Staying Behind Now Catches Up."[3] Baker tracked down a number of men who refused, evaded, or fled the Vietnam draft. Referred to throughout the article as draft dodgers or draft evaders, never as draft resisters, few of the men interviewed express pride or conviction about their decision not to fight in Vietnam, and *none* offers as a reason for his decision an unwillingness to kill Vietnamese. Most feel guilt, many ascribe their action to cowardice, one doubts his manhood: "The feelings people like me have are that maybe at a certain level I wasn't a real man because I never did what that guy who went to Vietnam did" (*SBCU* 3). Asked about his feeling toward the men who refused to serve, a Vietnam veteran explicitly identifies the Vietnam memorial and *Platoon* as the initiators of a change of attitude among draft resisters: "They have—I don't know if it's envy but I sense a feeling like that—a feeling like they had missed something. . . . [E]ver since the memorial and *Platoon,* a lot of people's minds seem to have changed. When people like that get to know you and they know you served, they say: 'Gee, maybe I should have done my part'" (*SBCU* 10). Another veteran, Arthur Egendorf, author of *Healing from the War*, reads the slogan, "Hell no! I won't go!" as an expression of "negativism" and argues that those who acted on it "identified themselves by negativism. . . . They are resigned to a sense of impotence," he adds, "committed to the ideal of no commitment" (*SBCU* 10). Though our literature of Vietnam insists on the brutalization of the American soldier in Vietnam, it insists even more persuasively that to refuse to undergo such brutalization is a morally bankrupt position.

There was, during the Vietnam War, a very different literary response based on the trip to Hanoi (for which Jane Fonda has yet to be forgiven by the many Vietnam veterans of Connecticut and western Massachusetts who mounted a campaign against her efforts to film parts of *Stanley and Iris* in their towns. "I'm not Fond'a Hanoi Jane" the bumper stickers read yet again in my neighborhood). Like most of the novels and films, this literature was documentary in inspiration, but the experience it sought to record was not that of the American soldier but that of the enemy. No doubt because of our preoccupation with the tragedy of the American soldier, our celebrated films and novels of Vietnam continue to offer a shockingly thin version of the Vietnamese, and a number of writers suspected, even while the war was still going on, that our failure to understand the first thing about the Vietnamese, about their history or their culture or their language or even their land, was very close to the heart of our problems in that country. Many of these writers were women, perhaps not surprisingly, since women had less access to and, perhaps, less commitment to the soldier's story. Denise Levertov's "Glimpses of Vietnamese Life," Susan Sontag's "Trip to Hanoi," Robin Morgan's "Four Visions on Vietnam," Frances Fitzgerald's *Fire in the Lake* all were efforts, in various forms, to create Vietnam as a culture in the American imagination and to confer upon the enemy a spiritual status at least equivalent, if not superior, to that of the American soldier. That this enterprise to represent the Vietnamese and their culture as the real victims of the tragedy of the war has all but dropped out of our sense of what the literature of Vietnam is all about is an indication, I think, of the sentimentalization, in the decades since Tet, of our imagination of the war.

The soldier's story, rooted as it is in a particular man's experience of a particular war, tends not only to sentimentalize, but also to dehistoricize our apprehension of war. Vietnam is not seen as one in a series of wars whose repetitions reveal a pattern in our relations with the peoples and cultures of the Third World. As in *Heart of Darkness*, which has been the paradigm for so many of our representations of Vietnam, the clash of cultures and of political and commercial interests is mythologized and psychologized into a kind of "ur" encounter of the white American man with his own unsuspected capacities for evil—Adam "surprised by sin"—a compelling story to be sure, but one that fails to represent that evil as *policy*, rendering it instead as an isolated and personal encounter that occurs only under extreme duress deep in the heart of the jungle. A more recent version of this same story is currently coming out of Israel and represents the Israeli soldier as surprised by sin in Gaza and the West Bank, thus transforming an occupying army into the victims of its own occupation.

Less myopic versions of our experience of Vietnam seem to me to occur primarily in literature we overlook in this context because we assume, consciously or unconsciously, that the soldier's story is the story of Vietnam. The tragic mutilation—in mind or body, or both—of the white American soldier in Vietnam has become axiomatic of our representations of that war. We seem unable to imagine, or recall, the war in any other terms. A portrait of an American soldier's experience of Vietnam akin, for example, to Doris Lessing's portrait of Douglas Knowell's experience of World War II in *A Proper Marriage* seems all but unthinkable. The plea for compassion, even admiration, for the soldier whose innocence has been so sorely tried, whose mind and body have been so indelibly scarred, is mercilessly parodied by Lessing in her rendering of Douglas Knowell's war adventures. Douglas is dying to get to World War II not because he has been duped by the romance of war or because he believes in the Allied cause. As a white Rhodesian, he cannot be whole-heartedly opposed to the racist Hitler, nor can he be wholeheart-edly sympathetic to the Communist Stalin. Douglas is delighted at the prospect of war because he is itching to get away from his pregnant wife. No hero, Douglas neither sins nor discovers sin on the battlefield; his ulcers keep him a thousand miles from even the nearest front in North Africa. And war introduces Douglas to no emotional intensities, leaves no tragic scars. When he isn't sexually harassing female army personnel, he passes his time in quarrels and fist fights with the rest of the army rejects, or in tearful bouts of self-pity. War makes no impression on Douglas Knowell, and he returns home only more committed to exerting in the civilian sphere the prerogatives he enjoys as a white man which he failed to exercise in the field of war.

The pervasiveness of the theme of the tragic mutilation of the white American soldier in Vietnam has driven such skeptical and ironic versions of soldiering from the field. It has also distracted our attention from the men, the policies, and the cultural pre-sumptions that sent American soldiers to Vietnam. The fall of Saigon, for example, is the event around which Joan Didion's *Democracy* circles, but its narrative is not about the American soldier "trapped by history, dragged down" etc., etc., but about the politicians, businessmen, and shady government officials—white American men too, just about every one of them—who devised and executed the policies that put the American soldier in the mud. Didion's is not a tale of innocent young men surprised (and why, *still*, so surprised?) by their capacities for violence and brutality and blinding fear, but of ripened war mongers, grown familiar and easy with their ways and means. War is the profession of the American men Didion depicts in *Democracy* and, by the end of the novel, our hearts do not bleed for them.

*Democracy* opens with Jack Lovett sharing with Inez Victor his recollection of the glorious spectacle of the dawn of the nuclear age:

The light at dawn during those Pacific tests was something to see.

Something to behold.

Something that could almost make you think you saw God, he said. . . .

He said: the sky was this pink no painter could approximate, one of the detonation theorists used to try, a pretty fair Sunday painter, he never got it. Just never captured it, never came close. The sky was this pink and the air was wet from the night rain, soft and wet and smelling like flowers, smelling like those flowers you used to pin in your hair when you drove out to Schofield, gardenias, the air in the morning smelled like gardenias, never mind there were not too many flowers around those shot islands.[4]

Jack Lovett claims no part in the devising or implementing of nuclear weapons. He was merely an observer, "Along for the ride. There for the show. You know me" (D 12). What is remarkable about his account of "those shots around 1952, 1953" (D 13) is the pure aesthetic delight, the unabashed pleasure he takes in the show. No memory of Hiroshima darkens the pink of the sky even the detonation theorist couldn't catch; no subsequent knowledge of the Cold War, the nuclear arms race, the Korean War, the Vietnam War, or the effects of nuclear radiation on the inhabitants of those shot islands casts a pall over Jack's enthusiasm for "those events in the Pacific. . . . Christ they were sweet" (D 13), he exclaims even in retrospect, as sweet as those evenings with which he confuses them, those evenings when Inez—"a little kid in high school" (D 14) then—pinned a gardenia in her hair and drove out to Schofield to see her war-lover.

"War-lover" is the name Inez's husband, Harry Victor, gives to Jack Lovett, intending the pun—Jack is Inez's lover in times of war, and he is a lover of war. Likable as Jack Lovett becomes in the course of the novel—largely because of the character of the competition—Jack is a dedicated and enthusiastic dealer in military information, technology, and weaponry. In 1955, when Inez marries Harry Victor and years before Harry cashes in politically on the Vietnam War, Jack Lovett is already supplanting the French in the militarization of Southeast Asia. He's in Saigon, setting up his Air Asia operation when he sends Inez the wedding present he won in a poker game there: a silver cigarette box engraved, "Résidence du Gouverneur Général de l'Indo-Chine" (D 88). In 1960, when Jack Lovett drops in on Inez at her job with *Vogue*, Inez knows he won't be staying long, "because he's running a little coup somewhere. I just bet" (D 33). For Jack, the continents of Asia and Africa have a very specific meaning: "Asia was ten thousand tanks here, three hundred Phantoms there. The heart of Africa was an enrichment facility" (D 35–36). Jack always has "various irons in the fire"; he's keeping "the usual balls in the air"; doing "a little business here and there" (D 38). And the irons in the fire, the balls in the air are invariably the implements of war.

War is Jack Lovett's business; he isn't for it or against it, he's simply a pro. The months before the fall of Saigon, Jack spends "shuttling between Saigon and Hong Kong and Honolulu" (D 151), transferring out of Vietnam

> the phantom business predicated on the perpetuation of the assistance effort. That there is money to be made in times of war is something we all understand abstractly. Fewer of us understand war itself as a specifically commercial enterprise, but Jack did, not abstractly but viscerally, and his overriding concern . . . had been to insure the covert survival of certain business interests. (D 151–52)

We never know, finally, whether Jack is what he calls "a state actor" or "a non-state actor" in the theater of war, and this, finally, is Joan Didion's point. Capitalism is the ideology of war in America, war as a business opportunity, a forum for the exchange of favors, a chance to put the right people together:

> There had been all the special assignments and the special consultancies and the special relationships in a fluid world where the collection of information was indistinguishable from the use of information and where national and private interests . . . did not collide but merged into a single pool of exchanged favors. (D 208)

"Wouldn't want your name on too many bottles around town" (D 40), is Jack Lovett's motto, and he embodies the covert forces of war in America—the vast, clandestine trade in military technology, arms, and information, which breeds the wars that sustain it. Harry Victor is, in many ways, Jack's antithesis. Harry is a politician, a public man for whom every occasion is a photo opportunity, a chance to enhance his image with the American electorate. But Harry, like Jack, sees war most essentially as a window of opportunity. A kind of essence of the Kennedy brothers and Eugene McCarthy all rolled into one, Harry Victor forges a political career out of antiwar protest. He is there at the sit-ins at Harvard and the Pentagon and Dow Chemical. At the Chicago convention in 1968, he has himself "photographed for *Life* getting tear-gassed in Grant Park" (*D* 48). And, when Harry is seeking the presidential nomination at the Miami convention in 1972, he claims to be "the voice of a generation that had taken fire on the battlefields of Vietnam and Chicago" (*D* 170). But, as Inez points out,

> you didn't start speaking for this generation until after the second caucus. You were only the voice of a generation that had taken fire on the battlefields of Vietnam and Chicago after you knew you didn't have the numbers. In addition to which. Moreover. Actually that was never your generation. Actually you were older. (*D* 170)

Harry lives for the numbers. His response to public and private catastrophe alike is, how will it play on the evening news? Joan Didion, speaking in the novel in her own voice of a course she offered at Berkeley in 1975 on "the idea of democracy in the work of certain post-industrial writers" (*D* 68), recalls suggesting to her class that they "consider the social organization implicit in the use of the autobiographical third person" (*D* 69). Harry Victor is the autobiographical third person, the media man endlessly reconstructed, edited, and revised for and by the public eye. "He's a congressman," Jack Lovett says of Harry in 1969 when he arrives with his family and entourage in Jakarta on a fact-finding mission, "Which means he's a radio actor" (*D* 99). And after Jack has tried unsuccessfully to convince Harry that Jakarta in 1969 is not the ideal spot for a family vacation, that the rioting and gun shots and grenades do not, as Harry insists, merely reflect "the normal turbulence of a nascent democracy" (*D* 95), Jack addresses Harry with uncharacteristic irritation and dislike: "You don't actually see what's happening in front of you. You don't see it unless you read it. You have to read it in the New York *Times*, then you start talking about it. Give a speech. Call for an investigation. Maybe you can come down here in a year or two, investigate what's happening tonight" (D 96–97). Years later, when Inez is asked in an interview what she regards as the major cost of public life, she answers, "Memory. . . . You jettison cargo. Eject crew. You *lose track*" (D 49). Harry Victor is a man curiously without memory, a man "who trots around the course wearing blinkers" (D 97), and who teaches his son, inevitably named Adlai, that the crux of the fall of Saigon "is finding a way to transfer anti-war sentiment to a multiple issue program" (D 163). The crux, of course, for Harry himself is finding a way to transfer antiwar sentiment to his senatorial campaign.

As the fall of Saigon is the event around which *Democracy* circles—not to measure its costs in human terms but to detail the political and economic machinations and realignments it necessitated—so Hawaii is the place to which the novel obsessively returns. In an early essay in *Slouching Towards Bethlehem*, Joan Didion identified the island paradise as having a peculiarly intimate relation with war: "it is war that is pivotal to the Hawaiian imagination, war that fills the mind, war that seems to hover over Honolulu like the rain clouds on Tantalus."[5] In *Democracy*, Hawaii is Inez's birthplace. It houses the U.S. military base she drives out to with gardenias in her hair to meet Jack Lovett between "shots." And when Saigon is about to fall, when planes from Vietnam are arriving steadily in Honolulu "bringing out the dependents, bringing out the dealers, bringing out the money, bringing out the pet dogs and the sponsored bar girls and the porcelain elephants" (D 15), Inez flies in from the opposite direction to watch her sister die and to learn that her daughter has hopped a plane to look for a job in Saigon. Hawaii is the transfer depot for the flotsam of war in Asia, but it is also the nerve center for the business of war in Asia. As Didion observes in the same essay in *Slouching Towards Bethlehem*,

> War is viewed with a curious ambivalence in Hawaii because the
> largest part of its population interprets war, however unconsciously,
> as a force for good, an instrument of social progress. And of course it
> was precisely World War II which cracked the spine of sugar feudal-
> ism, opened up a contracting economy and an immobile society,
> shattered forever the pleasant but formidable colonial world in
> which a handful of families controlled everything Hawaii did, where
> it shopped, how it shipped its goods, who could come in and how far
> they could go and at what point they would be closed out. (*STB* 198)

For Hawaii, too, war is a window of opportunity, and Inez's
uncle, Dwight Christian, the Jack Lovett of the island, does not
hesitate to use it.

Aptly named Christian, Inez's family belongs among that
handful of colonial families who once controlled everything. It is
a family "in which the colonial impulse had marked every member" (*D* 26). Flexible enough, however, to seize upon World War
II as a "specifically commercial enterprise," the Christian family
continues to thrive, not on sugar but on the government contracts and rising real estate values generated by the United States'
ongoing policy of political and military intervention in Asia.
Dwight Christian turns a pretty penny on his construction contracts at Long Binh and Cam Ranh Bay (contracts engineered by
the ubiquitous Jack Lovett), and he has no qualms about using
the second-generation Japanese immigrant Wendell Omura to
squeeze his own brother-in-law "out of windward Oahu and
coincidentally out of the container business" (*D* 26). Though the
Christian women tend to look back on the years of World War II
with some regret—Inez's grandmother recalls the fun she used to
have with the polo-playing generals out at Schofield, and Inez's
sister, Janet, recollects the "marvelous simple way of life that you
might describe as gone with the wind" (*D* 65)—Janet's nostalgia
does not impede the progress of her affair with Wendell Omura,
and Dwight Christian positively welcomes the opportunity the
profits of war accord him to play "every Robert Trent Jones golf
course in the world" (*D* 26). Only Janet and Inez's father, Paul
Christian, seems unable to adjust to the new and thriving, war-
spawn Hawaii. A kind of colonial *manqué*, Paul drifts around the

world in search of "that marvelous simple way of life" to which he feels entitled. When he returns to Hawaii to discover Janet's affair with the scion of the Nisei family that has wrested its share of power from that handful of white colonial families who once controlled everything, Paul shoots both his daughter and the man he refers to as "the Oriental."

The war victims in this novel are not American soldiers. Though Jack Lovett comes home in a body bag, he dies not of war wounds but of an attack of the heart. The war victims here are the wives, daughters, and lovers of the war profiteers. Janet falls victim to a father who, crazed by the loss of his colonial privilege, is still fighting World War II. Jessie, the daughter of Inez and Harry Victor, meanders from one troubled Third World capital to another, in an effort to ignore the agenda of her father, her brother, and American politicians in general, whom she summarily dismisses as "assholes" (D 163). Inez, when she belatedly ceases "to claim the American exemption" and discovers "that the comfortable entrepreneurial life of an American colony" does not necessarily represent "a record of individual triumphs over a hostile environment" (D 201), can place herself, like her daughter, only among the refugees, those who measure the cost of American foreign policy in the loss not of dollars and American soldiers, but of health, family, home, native land, and culture. Inez spends her days in the administration of "what are by now the dozen refugee camps around Kuala Lumpur" (D 222). While she still considers herself "an American national" (though not, apparently, an American citizen), she vows to remain in Kuala Lumpur until the last refugee is dispatched, to be, in other words, the last of the last refugees.

While Didion turns our attention from American losses to American profits in Vietnam and suggests that the war there was perhaps more costly and profoundly alienating to American women than it was to American men, she still presents the war as an essentially American tragedy and measures its impact in terms of the disintegration of American culture. An even more capacious exploration of war, not just of the Vietnam War but of the wars that have recurred with obsessive regularity throughout this century, occurs, I think, in the fiction of Doris Lessing. Lessing is one of the few novelists of the generation that spans World War I to the present to fix her eyes on the history of human violence in our time. Born in 1919 of a World War I amputee and his nurse, and coming of age with the outbreak of World War II, Lessing recognized early that hers was a generation and a culture steeped in war. Of her intention in her first series of novels, *Children of Violence*, written mainly in the fifties, Lessing says: "I think the title explains what I essentially want to say. I want to explain what it is like to be a human being in a century when you open your eyes on war and on human beings disliking each other."[6] One of Lessing's crucial contributions here to the literature of war is her intuitive expansion of its terrain. War is not something a handful of doomed young men trip over in the jungles of an alien and inhospitable land; war is what the sons and daughters of Europe and America wake up to every day, it's the marrow of our culture.

In *Children of Violence*, Lessing treats war as a family legacy, it's something Dad hands down to son, Mom hands down to daughter. Focusing, as the series does, on World War I and World War II, conveniently precisely a generation apart, Lessing treats the battlefield and home as different arenas of the same conflict. Marxist historical determinism and Freudian psychological determinism join hands to force her generation to repeat the war of its parents. Her generation is, in fact, a direct product of war, and metaphors of violence and conflict shape its understanding not just of the relations between nations and races, but also of the relations between men and women, between parents and children. The Cold War, the War between the Sexes, the War between the Generations are merely the domestic names for the mentality that erupts militarily under the names of World War I, World War II, Korea, Vietnam, Afghanistan, Nicaragua.

Vietnam, of course, fits very neatly into this generational pattern of violence. Heating up almost exactly twenty years after the end of World War II—Iwo Jima plus twenty, we might even say—Vietnam was fought on both sides of the world largely by the sons and daughters of the soldiers and nurses of World War II, and what's at the back of our minds, if not on the tip of our tongues, when we say "Tet plus twenty," what makes this date reverberate with a peculiar significance, is not just our sense that it's time for a retrospective, it's also our sense that it's time for another war. Many American writers on Vietnam share this sense of the war as an inheritance, the legacy of the World War II generation to its children. I heard Chuck Norris, father of *Missing in Action, I, II, and III,* say on TV that John Wayne was like a father to him. And in *Going after Cacciato,* Paul Berlin goes to Vietnam largely because his father can imagine no other possible response to "the call of duty." Like the protagonists of *The Deer Hunter,* Paul Berlin is groomed for war in his boyhood by participating with his father in the war game called hunting. This confusion of war with sport is, in fact, a kind of trope of the imagination of the American soldier in Vietnam, and in a country in which we conduct football games, presidential elections, video games, foreign policy, disarmament talks, children's cartoons, and sexual relations in the rhetoric of the prize fight, we might consider whether the bellicosity of our metaphors doesn't have something to do with our ever-readiness for war.

In part because she is a daughter of the British, not a son of the American empire, Lessing does not present Vietnam as the war that confirms a pattern of generational violence. From the point of view of Europe, Vietnam is not so special. Vietnam is merely one more in a series of violent clashes along the perimeters of the spheres of influence of the super powers. Moreover, Lessing has come to regard her view of war as a family affair as excessively deterministic, permitting no response but an enlightened cynicism. The quotation from Lewis Carroll that Lessing puts at the beginning of the second volume of *Children of Violence* hints at her early recognition of the dangers of even a wry and witty fatalism: "'You shouldn't make jokes,' Alice said, 'if it makes you so unhappy.'"[7] In her recent fiction, Lessing has taken a much more global and impersonal view of Vietnam in particular, and of war in this century in general. In *Shikasta,* the first volume of her *Canopus in Argos* series, Lessing presents the history of the earth from prehistory to the not-so-distant future through the eyes of a vastly superior species from another galaxy. This view robs Vietnam of the special case status we Americans tend to give it, and places it instead inside a pattern of violence perpetuated, not by Communists against the "free world," but by the white races against the nonwhite races of the world.

We enter *Shikasta* through the eyes of Johor, a member of the Canopean Colonial Service who has a life expectancy of 60,000 years and who has been an occasional emissary to Shikasta (to Canopeans, "the broken one"; to us, Earth) over a period of many thousands of years. Johor's current mission will take him to Shikasta in the late twentieth century, a century defined by the long view the novel takes of our history as "the Century of Destruction." But before entering Shikasta, an experience Johor anticipates with dismay and dread, he recollects a previous visit to the planet "in the First Time, when . . . [it] was a glory and a hope of Canopus."[8] Johor's recollections take him back to "the Time of the Giants," a prehistoric period in the evolution of the earth when two species—the Giants and the Natives—thrive in a symbiotic relationship. Though the Giants are twice the size of the Natives and intellectually and culturally far more advanced, they have established with the Natives "a tutelary relation which [gives] the liveliest of interest and satisfaction to both sides" (S 17). Johor recalls entering The Round City, a city shared by Giants and Natives, alert for signs of what he knows as the Degenerative Disease. Although this disease manifests itself physically in a shrinking life span, it is essentially a disease of the soul or moral fibre of a species and it invariably expresses itself as an assumption of superiority. Johor scrutinizes the architecture of the city for "the grandiosities and pomps" (S 32) symptomatic of the disease, but he finds nothing of the kind:

> When I came out into the one central area, where the public buildings stood, made of the same golden-brown stone, all was harmony and proportion. Not in this city could it be possible for a child being brought by its parents to be introduced to the halls, towers, centres of its heritage, to feel awed and alienated, to know itself a nothing, a little frightened creature who must obey, and watch for Authority. . . . on the contrary, anyone walking here,

among these welcoming warm-colored buildings, must feel only the closeness, the match, between individual and surroundings. (S 32)

Johor himself is in the form of a Native, and he approaches a pair of Giants with some trepidation: "I was never ready to be less than wary about the relations between tutors and taught" (S 33). But when the Giants catch sight of him, they "at once smiled and nodded—and were still prepared to move off, showing that they did not expect either side to be in need of the other" (S 33). When Johor enters a Giants' building, he is quickly provided with a Native-sized chair, table, and bed in a room commeasurate with his proportions, and when he meets with the Giants, they sit on the floor and he sits on a pile of rugs, "adjusted so that our faces were at the same level" (S 37). Through such a painstaking reading of details of manners and spatial arrangements, Johor creates for the reader an experience of a culture in which even a radical advantage in physical strength and intellectual prowess asserts no claim to superior status or social privilege. The Giants' incapacity to perceive themselves as superior or more deserving even makes them incapable of grasping the meaning of the word "enemy": "The word fled by them, unmarked, it did not strike a home in them anywhere" (S 36).

The Giants and the Natives offer the reader a glimpse of a culture not only without war but also without the structures of consciousness that breed war. The glimpse is short-lived; even as we are introduced to it, the culture of the Giants and the Natives is disintegrating, and when Johor returns to Shikasta in the twentieth century, it is lost even to memory. The culture that thrived "in peace, mutual help, aspirations for more of the same" (S 22) has succumbed to the culture of a singularly bellicose breed "characterized by a peculiar insensitivity to the merits of other cultures, an insensitivity quite unparalleled in previous history" (S 83). This breed, "a particularly arrogant and self-satisfied breed, a minority of the minority white race, dominate[s] most of Shikasta, a multitude of different races, cultures, and religions which, on the whole, [are] superior to that of the oppressors" (S 83). Antithetical to the Giants, who failed even to comprehend such concepts as "superior" and "enemy," this breed fails to comprehend anything else, and therefore devotes all its resources to war. Though most late twentieth-century inhabitants of Shikasta console themselves with a view of war as something that comes and goes, numbering their wars as though peace prevails in between, they are, in fact, living in an era in which "the governing factor [is] . . . the need for war, as such" (S 89). Successive wars have so consolidated the power of the military, the arms industry, and the scientific community that their interests alone dictate the form, timing, and intensity of warfare: "Again the armament industries flourished, and [World War II] . . . finally established them as the real rulers of every geographical area" (S 86). But the deepest damage has been done to the minds of Shikastans by the incessant propaganda required to make them believe that the waste, the wreckage, and the horror they see everywhere around them is not what it seems: "Above all, the worst wounds were inflicted in the very substance, the deepest minds, of the people themselves. Propaganda in every area, by every group, was totally unscrupulous, vicious, lying— and self-defeating—because in the long run, people could not believe the truth when it came their way" (S 86).

Lessing's account of contemporary white Western culture from the outside bears a striking resemblance to Didion's account of contemporary American culture from the inside. To Didion's account, however, Lessing adds a critique of our representations of war. Our capacity to "forget" between wars the "submersion in the barbaric, the savage, the degrading" (S 89) which war most essentially is, is a product of our peculiar construction of our memories of war: "Heroisms and escapes and braveries of local and limited kinds were raised into national preoccupations, which were in fact forms of religion. But this not only did not assist, but prevented, an understanding of how the fabric of cultures had been attacked and destroyed" (S 89). Our dominant literature of Vietnam, stressing as it does "heroisms and escapes and braveries of local and limited kinds," is an act, then, not of remembering but of forgetting war. It feeds our desire to "relegate war—and its consequences—into something that happened elsewhere and did not affect [us]; or something that had happened to [us], but between such and such dates, and then taken itself off" (S 232).

With Johor's return to Shikasta at the end of the Century of Destruction, the novel moves from an account of our unrecorded past to an account of our unrecordable future. But "coming events cast their shadows before" (S 231), and we can discern in our present many shadows of Lessing's future. The Children's Camps, for example, are strikingly reminiscent of the West Bank Palestinian schools described by David Grossman in *The Yellow Wind*, and the recurrent outbreaks of lethal contagious diseases inevitably bring the AIDS epidemic to mind. Johor returns to a world in which militarization has penetrated deep into the fabric of civilian life. The new technologies have created massive unemployment, particularly among the young:

> Already the cities were helpless before the aimless, random, unorganized violence characteristic of small groups of the young, male and female, who "for no reason" destroyed anything they could. . . . The remedy, an increase in policing—a general increase in militarisation, in fact—was already highlighting the nature of the problem. What is begun has a momentum: the consequences of greater police surveillance, sharper penalties, and the further cramming of prisons already overfull, must be even greater police surveillance and powers, sharper penalties, and a criminal population becoming steadily more brutalized. (S 232)

The ultimate solution to a dilemma we see even today played out nightly on the evening news is the militarization of youth. By the time of Johor's return, youth armies under civilian designations cover the globe and are already beginning to take command of themselves.

In the political sphere, seeds planted in our present have also taken root and flourished. China is in the ascendancy and is attempting to consolidate its sway by provoking the dark races against the white race, already weakened and decimated by the fruits of its colonial policies and the poisons of its new technologies. China's ultimate intention is the genocide of the white race and the occupation of Europe and North America, and it is this intention that Johor is dispatched to Shikasta to subvert.

Johor is born on Earth as George Sherban, the son of parents who appear white but whose racial lineage is, in fact, mixed (his grandmother is Indian; his grandfather is a Polish Jew, probably descended from the Khazars). In appearance, George is dark-haired and olive-skinned—white but off-white—and he is raised in North Africa, a borderland between the light and dark races. His education is singular. As his sister, Rachel, notes in her journal, "I work for exams . . . George doesn't work for exams. What he does is this. Wherever we go he attends college or university or something. Or tutors come. Or he goes off on trips with Father and Mother. . . . But he doesn't take exams" (S 251). Later, Rachel recognizes why George doesn't take exams:

> During the term when George was doing the History of the Religions of the Middle East at the Madrasa, he also took courses from a Christian and from a Jew. In other words, while he was learning the curriculum, he was simultaneously learning the partisan points of view that wouldn't be in the curriculum. . . . That means he couldn't take exams, because what he had learned would never be contained in the exam questions. . . . *He is being educated for something different.* (S 254)

Literally, George is being educated to save the white race; metaphorically, he is being educated to baffle the categorical impulse, the impulse at the root of our bellicosity to pen human beings within arbitrary, mutually exclusive, and hostile boundaries (the impulse that bears such strange fruit in South Africa today). Thus, it is no surprise when we discover George, at one point in the novel, simultaneously representing the Jewish Guardians of the Poor, the Islamic Youth Federation for the Care of the Cities, and the United Christian Federation of Young Functionaries for Civil Care.

Most profoundly, George's education is an education in peace-making, and it bears fruit at "The Trial," which culminates the novel. Though the trial is a symbolic event staged by the youth armies of the world, the fate of the white race in fact hangs in the balance. On trial for its life for its crimes against the dark races, the white race faces literal extinction if the verdict goes against it. Only George Sherban's brilliant orchestration of the event prevents a genocidal, global race war.

George's tactics, then, bear careful scrutiny, since they provide a model of how to wrest peace from the jaws of war. Everything about the staging of the trial portends disaster. The site is Greece, the cradle of Western civilization, a site bound to provoke rage in the hearts of the colonized. Both spectators and participants are predominantly young people—volatile, restless, hungry, disinherited, and representative of every warring faction on the face of the earth. Food and water are in short supply, accommodations are abysmal, most delegates from both Europe and the emergent nations arrive half-starved and in rags, anticipation of a "final solution" is intense. The amphitheatre in which the trial is staged is too small for the multitudes, the heat of the day is unendurable, witnesses can be heard only if the crowd keeps perfect silence.

Out of conditions begging for a blood bath, George Sherban's mission is to construct peace. He succeeds by a series of maneuvers that are breath-taking in their simplicity, far-reaching in their effects. First, he turns day into night, conducting the trial by torchlight and moonlight from dark to dawn. The torches, which mute all racial distinctions, are maintained by "the inheritors," the youngest children at the trial, so those only a decade or so older can never for an instant forget how quickly they will be supplanted, how soon they will be held accountable for the world they have bequeathed to the next generation.

George Sherban's singular education has led to his election as representative of the dark races. He, a white man, is to prosecute their case against the white race. Always, he is attended by children of every race. For the defense, an old white English man, John Brent-Oxford, has been selected, and always he is accompanied by George's brother, Benjamin, and two children, one white, one jet black. The spectators are similarly intermingled; no group is segregated by race, gender, or nationality, except the Chinese, who are "put prominently and distinctively in a bloc in the very best position, low down and halfway between the two groups. This was the only national group which was allotted a special position and marked with a banner—the only one, in other words, to which attention was directed throughout the 'Trial' " (S 318). The first witness George calls against the white race is also Chinese, a well-fed, neatly dressed, healthy-looking young woman. Both the well-fed Chinese woman and the special treatment accorded to the Chinese delegation draw attention to the new claimants to superiority and privilege, thus diffusing the hostility between black and white—between the representatives of the emergent nations and of Europe—both of whom recognize their own emaciation in the faces of the other. Though witness after witness—a Native American, a South American Indian, a Zimbabwean, a Vietnamese—indicts the white race for its history of contempt, brutality, stupidity, exploitation, and barbaric aggression against the nonwhite peoples of the world, the only clear-cut, unambiguous target for their indignation remains the Chinese bloc.

Witnesses for the prosecution testify for eight nights, but soon interest shifts from the formal hearings to the informal gatherings which occur during the intersessions—the discussion groups, debates, seminars, and spontaneous conversations at which George Sherban and his adversary, John Brent-Oxford, are ubiquitous presences. Friendships and love affairs cross racial boundaries, a thirst for revenge arising quite justifiably from a history of racial oppression is supplanted by a common recognition of the present peril that threatens the entire human race.

On the ninth night, George Sherban announces quite casually that the prosecution rests its case. John Brent-Oxford, for the defense, speaks for the first time: "I plead guilty to everything that has been said. How can I do anything else?" (S 335). In defense of the white race, he offers only a question: "Why is it that you, the accusers, have adopted with such energy and efficiency the ways you have been criticizing? . . . Why is it that so many of you who have not been forced into it, have chosen to copy the materialism, the greed, the rapacity of the white man's technological society?" (S 335). On this query, George Sherban adjourns the session, and when the trial reconvenes after four hours of energetic discussion in "hundreds of conversations between couples, among groups, in 'seminars'" (S 336), George steps forward to say, "Yesterday, the accused made a counteraccusation. It is one that has been thought about and discussed ever since. But today I want to put forward a self-criticism" (S 336). The self-criticism George proposes to the dark races he represents is of the treatment of the Untouchables in India:

> For three thousand years India has persecuted and ill-treated a part of its own population. . . . This is not a question of a year's oppression, a decade's oppression, a century's ill-treatment, not the results of a short-lived and unsuccessful regime like the British Empire, not a ten-year outburst of savagery like Hitler's regime in Europe, not fifty years of savagery like Russian communism, but something built into a religion and a way of life, a culture, so deeply embedded that the frightfulness and ugliness of it cannot even be observed by the people who practice it. (S 337)

On this anticlimactic note of self-criticism, the trial of the white race ends, not with a decision to exterminate all the brutes—to apply Kurtz's solution to the real culprits—but with the admonition to search out the enemy in ourselves. The assumption of superiority is not an intrinsic characteristic of any race, sex, or nationality; it is a potential within us all which, when cultivated, becomes the motivating force behind aggression and exploitation, race being a central, but certainly not the only, category in which it expresses itself. Thus, the trial of black against white—the ultimate agon of a culture of bellicosity—peters out, the delegates scatter over the world, and nothing more is heard of what "was on the cards, . . . a determined and planned wiping out of the remaining European populations" (S 340).

In *The Remasculinization of America: Gender and the Vietnam War*, Susan Jeffords traces, in our representations of the Vietnam War in literature and film over the last decade and a half, the resurrection of the Vietnam veteran and his displacement of the radical as the arbiter of that war's meaning. She regards this transformation as emblematic of a "regeneration of the projects of patriarchy."[9] Our memories of the Vietnam War have become not only the exclusive property of veterans, but also "the occasion for announcing the primacy of bonds between men" (RA 99). But Jeffords herself perpetuates the privilege of the veteran to construct our memories of war by attending only to his account. Historically, war has always been a patriarchal project, and unless we undermine the soldier's monopoly on representing himself at war, our memories of war will overtly or covertly serve his interests. We can challenge this monopoly only by redefining what war literature is about. As Marge Piercy makes clear in *Gone to Soldiers*, war is not something experienced only by men with guns on the battlefield. War presses the entire fabric of civilian life into service. Though we see few monuments or memorials to them, and hear even fewer tales of their heroism or of their tragic defeat, women and children and civilian men die as horribly in war as do the men with the guns, and in far greater numbers. Moreover, as Didion insists in *Democracy*, the white American veteran's story of his suffering in the jungles of Vietnam must not blind us to the enormous profits accrued in the course of that war by other, more fortunate members of the American political and military establishment, whose interests the veteran, however benightedly, consented to serve.

But Lessing, above all, forces us to examine the extreme narrowness of the memory of war engendered by our inclination to listen only to soldiers. The long view of war in this century that Lessing takes in *Shikasta*—a view that refuses to allow us for a moment to take consolation in the illusion that war is something that happened then, or over there, or to them—forces us to acknowledge that war has infected our deepest understanding of ourselves and our world in this century. It has become an assumption of our culture, it has taken root in our feelings, it shapes our habitual responses to our nearest and dearest, as well as to those most alien and distant from us. In an interview in the *New York Times* in 1988, Lessing speaks of how war wound its tentacles around her own heart:

I do have a sense, and I've never not had it, of how easily things can vanish. . . . It's a sense of disaster. I know where it comes from—my upbringing. That damn First World War, which rode my entire childhood, because my father was so damaged by it. This damn war rammed down my throat day and night, and then World War II coming, which they talked about all the time. You know, you never can get out from under this kind of upbringing, the continual obsession with this. And after all, it's true. These wars did arise, and destroyed a beautiful household with all the loving children. [10]

None of us wants war rammed down our throats, but can we afford to deny the truth that it has been? George Sherban's education nurtured in him the vision and the imagination to create a process that transforms the bellicosity we have swallowed into self-criticism, that replaces our conviction of our superiority with a recognition of the frightfulness and ugliness deeply embedded in ourselves and our culture. But in the United States, we no longer seek the solution to problems in our own wrong thinking and wrong doing; we declare war on them. Drugs, poverty, AIDS, teenage pregnancy, cancer are not enemies we can kill with guns and tanks and bombs, but rather than question our metaphors, we turn our guns on the poor, the addicted, and the homosexual.

## NOTES

1. Doris Lessing, *The Golden Notebook* (New York, 1973), 437. Hereafter referred to as *TGN*.
2. Patricia Holt, "Viet Vet Sees War As a Moral Vacuum," *San Francisco Chronicle*, January 1988.
3. Bob Baker, "Staying Behind Catches Up," *Los Angeles Times*, February 22, 1988. Hereafter referred to as *SBCU*.
4. Joan Didion, *Democracy* (New York, 1984), 11. Hereafter referred to as *D*.
5. Joan Didion, *Slouching Towards Bethlehem* (New York, 1979), 203. Hereafter referred to as *STB*.
6. Doris Lessing, *A Small Personal Voice* (New York, 1975), 57.
7. Doris Lessing, *A Proper Marriage* (New York, 1970), 1.

8. Doris Lessing, *Shikasta* (New York, 1979), 14. Hereafter referred to as *S*.

9. Susan Jeffords, *The Remasculinization of America: Gender and the Vietnam War* (Bloomington, 1989). Hereafter referred to as *RA*.

10. Mervyn Rothstein, "The Painful Nurturing of Doris Lessing's 'Fifth Child,'" *New York Times*, June 14, 1988, C21.

## War Torn

Ten years after Elizabeth left for the mountains, we got the announcement of the birth of her daughter. "May she become a flourishing hidden tree, That all her thoughts may like the linnet's be," the printed card said. We thought Elizabeth must be joking.

But we couldn't be sure. These were the first words we'd heard from Elizabeth since she left for the Sierras in the spring of 1975 after watching Saigon fall all night on TV. She slipped away, left nothing behind but a tiny enamel red star pinned to a tatter of an army-green jacket, and a note that said, "Found on the volley ball court, People's Park 1969. Gone to the Sierras." For all we knew, this Elizabeth was a different person.

A woman sits on a suitcase marked U.S. Property outside the fence at Tan Son Nhut airport. Her back is straight, her legs are crossed, a shoe without a heel dangles from one toe. From this distance it looks like a fur collar around her shoulders, odd garb for this season in Saigon, though not necessarily for this moment, and then the camera zooms in and we see it is a baby around her shoulders. The sky has been quiet for hours. She will be found in the morning and sent north. In ten years she will be a different person.

When we realized Elizabeth was gone, naturally we asked ourselves why she had been so severe with us, her family, her tribe. She wasn't the only one to leave us after the war, but she was the most thorough.

At the embassy they are packing paper. Paper is everywhere, it drifts down empty halls through empty doorways into empty rooms, it pops out of overstuffed bags, it lies like corpses in piles under open windows. The embassy will never get all its paper out, never shred all its history.

Not that the war was over, not that men, women, and children weren't still dying in Vietnam, Cambodia, and Laos in the same staggering numbers and positions that had so arrested us when we first came across them in *Life*. Not that any of us left Berkeley clinging to the wheels of a cargo plane, though we could use such an image now for our state of mind. Except for Elizabeth we left Berkeley deliberately, with new plans for the future now that the war was over, not that the war was over.

She runs across the tarmac shedding like a tree in a big wind in October. First her bundles rip from her hands and shoulders. Her pocketbook goes with her jacket. Ornaments in her hair tear loose, she kicks off her shoes. Her skirt rips to her thigh, her blouse flies opens. She looks as if she means to rise naked as a bird off that tarmac.

Elizabeth was going to the mountains, we figured at the time, to survey the damage. Not that Berkeley was deeply scarred. From above, you'd never know there'd been a war here. No rubble, no sandbags, no tunnels, no bomb craters. The town, cradled between bay and hills, glimmered pink in the sun against a turquoise sky, just as it always had.

Elizabeth went, of course, to American mountains. Had Berkeley been Saigon, the mountains would not have been green. Had the Central Valley been the Plain of Jars, the mountains would have been littered with crater lakes and live guava, pineapple, and orange cluster bombs. But being American, the mountains were breathtaking and relatively un-molested, and the sky was as safe as it's been since 1945.

The sky is not safe as they race across the tarmac at Tan Son Nhut the day Saigon falls. People are falling out of it, and money and guns and babies and boots. Nobody is holding on to more than her life and nobody looks up where the blades of the copters slice indiscriminately what falls from and what rises to the sky.

We wondered if Elizabeth would sleep in the place we'd all slept together in 1969, the place where we were hustled up be-fore daybreak by five Weathermen with guns. We were found and destroyed, they informed us, then stayed to drink coffee and show off their guns and army shovels and educate us about survival in the wilderness. They were establishing headquar-ters, making maps, burying stashes.

We don't see the enemy the day Saigon falls, we see only our-selves driving up to the planes in fancy cars with military es-corts, boarding the planes like we do at Kennedy or Heathrow with only a few hairs out of place. We know there is an enemy from the way our Vietnamese friends run all over each other and hang from airplane wheels to get away, but what we actu-ally see for an instant on the other side of the fence around Tan Son Nhut is a child, hooked with frozen fingers, hanging dazed and abandoned, then the camera zooms in to the wheel of the plane we Americans have just boarded with so few hairs out of place, where a man curls like a snail around the hub, so we never see the reflection in the child's eyes of the events on the tarmac.

Since the war was over and there wasn't going to be any fight-ing in the Sierras, we didn't suppose Elizabeth had gone to the mountains to join the People's Army, though the idea gave us pleasure. The enamel red star brought the same scene to all our minds. It was three or four weeks after Ronald Reagan had put up the ten-foot chain-link fence around People's Park. One person had died, a filmmaker had been blinded, there'd been a lot of tear gas and buckshot and billyclub wounds, and thirty thousand had arrived the week before to demonstrate. But now the national guard was gone, and Ronald Reagan had put in the volley-ball courts, and things were quiet around the park except at night, when an angry crowd gathered to press in, press in against the fence. On the other side, the Alameda sheriffs cavorted in helmets and flack jackets. The park was lit up like a living room, and the sheriffs were waving their guns around as they took turns on the only swing set they hadn't broken, and bounced up and down on the seesaw. Somebody lobbed a stink bomb into the far corner of the park and as the cops took off, we heard Elizabeth say, "I'm over," and over the fence she went, leaping into the floodlights like a dancer. She was laughing as she ran to the volley-ball net and cut it down, and she might not have been spotted at all, so swift and sure she was of her part, had she not paused to pick something up from the court. But she was over the fence before the sheriff caught up with her and he chose not to shoot. We scolded her afterward, but secretly we called her our street-fighting woman, and we liked to think of her picking up the gun for us all.

There's shooting around Tan Son Nhut, of course, the day Saigon falls, but shooting seems a natural way to die, compared to falling out of the sky. And we have seen more unusual shootings, shootings where the gun is raised to the skull, cocked and triggered without the flicker of a thought between the cocking and the letting go. Shootings we see only the remains of, but hear graphically described by boys and girls stashed in tunnels, ferreted out by the cameras and microphones that always let us know what's going on. Shooting at Tan Son Nhut that day seems the natural way to go.

We favored the speculation that Elizabeth would take the same path to the same place we had camped in 1969 in search of

our protection or, more modestly, our company. We had not
been good company in recent years, we had not been a family,
a tribe. We talked about how we were falling apart as we finished up our degrees, but the discussions were listless and we
acted alone.

But none so alone as Elizabeth, we agreed, after months
rolled by and we realized she wasn't coming home. She had
left as much with us as she meant to leave, we guessed, until
we got the package from Montana with the gun inside,
wrapped up in the red bandana she used to wear against tear
gas in the streets. It was the bandana that took us all back to
the Sierras in '69, and Elizabeth, the streak of red around her
neck like a gash above the sleek brown tan of her back and
thighs, leaping through the hoops of Waterwheel Falls. She
lands on a slippery rock, rolls around a couple times in the icy
water and comes up laughing. And why our minds turned then
to Berkeley and the night Saigon fell, none of us is sure, but
we all recalled as one that moment on the porch of Elizabeth's
place when she finally opened the door. She was naked and
she sounded half-dead when she said she didn't want any company, ever.

The orphans are packed in a fly-by-night, CIA charter plane. It
is estimated they will more than pay their way when they are
sold in the states. They are packed in the hold with the jeeps
and antiaircraft guns. As the plane lumbers down the runway it
seems nothing can lift it into the sky, so swollen and sick is its
belly, but it rises and flies halfway to Guam before it goes down
in the Pacific almost unnoticed, so heavy is the traffic over the
Pacific that day.

We don't know why Elizabeth has sent us the announcement,
why she has broken her silence to inform us of the birth of her
daughter. We have pondered the lines from Yeats but can
come to no conclusion. We piece together fragments, rumors,
uncertain glimpses. One of us has a color photo of a charming
New England house in a profusion of spring flowers: tulips,

phlox, forsythia, lilacs, dogwood and cherry trees. It's said to be her house, but we can't be sure. One of us claims she is among a group of women arrested at the launching of a Trident submarine in Groton, but the newspaper photo is blurred and the woman looks too heavy. We trust she has a daughter, but if she keeps her daughter from the thoughts that severed her from us, we cannot know.

A young girl runs naked from a pagoda we have bombed. Her clothes are napalmed from her body and her charred arms stretch out and she cannot see that no one is there, she can only feel the flames which are consuming the pagoda behind her consuming the temple of herself.

She lives in America now. Her scars hardly showed when she was interviewed on TV not long ago. She said she blames no one, she hates war.

# War and

# Postmodern Memory

> I have a young daughter and we live in the Pioneer Valley in western Massachusetts. The best equipped playground in this valley so devoted to the education of the young that it is known in Washington as "The Happy Valley" happens to be at Westover Air Force Base. The playground was built by bomber pilots for their children, and it is a small city of slides and jungle gyms and rings and bars and mazes and tank tire tunnels. When we go there, the same pilots who so lovingly constructed it circle lazily overhead, ready to follow orders which would turn it and their children to dust.

In 1938, when Virginia Woolf published *Three Guineas*—one of the most elegant feminist critiques of war ever written—most of the men she cared for were miffed. Her nephew, Quentin Bell, and her good friends E. M. Forster and Maynard Keynes were at best enraged, at worst coolly contemptuous, and even her husband was less enthusiastic than Woolf thought he ought to be. Why this sense of impropriety, oddness, outrage even, when a woman involves herself and her sex in a discussion of war? We are at risk, after all. Though we are not yet being drafted or sent into combat in Nicaragua or Libya or the Middle East, men's weapons have too wide and indiscriminate an embrace for us to rely on them for our protection. As Virginia Woolf observed in 1938, when men's weapons had a far narrower reach, "any kitchenmaid . . . can read and understand the meaning of 'Air Raid Precautions' when written in large letters upon a blank wall . . . [and] any kitchenmaid would attempt to construe a passage in Pindar if told that her life depended on it."[1]

Women are robbed of the authority to express themselves on the subject of war because they are assumed not to be in war. *Men without Women*, Hemingway called his collection of World War II stories, and though we all agree that Norman Mailer's *Naked and the Dead* belongs in the genre of the war novel, I have rarely seen Doris Lessing's *Children of Violence* series so labeled. In his disturbing article, "Why Men Love War," William Broyles, Jr., presents his idea of the archetypal war story, one he found in Michael Herr's *Dispatches:* "Patrol went up the mountain. One man came back. He died before he could tell us what happened." As Broyles points out, the purpose of this story is "not to enlighten but to exclude." Its message is, "I suffered, I was there. You were not. Only these facts matter."[2]

This assumption of women's absence from the field of battle permits literary criticism to remain unabashedly sexist on the subject of war. As the first essay in this collection points out, even such "definitive" studies of the literature of World War I as Paul Fussell's *Great War and Modern Memory* disregard the work of women. Fussell's oversight is perhaps comprehensible, given the relative simplicities of the war he was remembering. In World War I, the "front" was clearly delineated and English and American women could choose to stay behind it, though a remarkable number didn't. Gertrude Stein, Edith Wharton, Vera Brittain, Radclyffe Hall, and Winifred Holtby all were there, as were the many less noted women who served in signal, motorcycle, and nursing corps. Even World War II had its limits, and though huge civilian populations in Europe and Japan died, the myth of a protected zone for women and children survived. In modern guerrilla warfare, however, the front is difficult to find, the rear is not necessarily any safer, and being a woman or a civilian is no guarantee of exemption.

Modern nuclear warfare, of course, vaporizes the myth of a protected zone, of woman's exclusion from war, yet military science remains as pronouncedly masculine as the combat zone. War and its kindred sciences divide the sexes in Western culture more radically than any other human activities, with the exception of childbearing and, possibly, sports. The breathtaking maleness of the terrains of both the military and its symbiotic sciences and technologies, of even the terrain of protest against the military and these sciences and technologies, is what first impresses most women writers bold enough to assert an opinion on these matters. That there is a connection between this radical separation of men from women and children and the release of mental and physical impulses of pure destruction is a suspicion most women writers on war find impossible to dismiss.

So Woolf's "attempt to involve a discussion of women's rights with the far more agonizing and immediate question of what we [are] to do in order to meet the ever-growing menace of Fascism and [now, nuclear] war"[3] is not, for most women writers, odd but inevitable. Once we move beyond the bartering of hardware to an analysis of the human type that produces, disseminates, and uses the hardware, that type stands forth sharply as a man who has reduced his intellectual, social, and physical commitments to women and children to a minimum, or who, at least, is prepared to do so upon command.

In the military, as Cynthia Enloe convincingly demonstrates in *Does Khaki Become You?*, a willingness to forsake wife and family is painstakingly inculcated in the soldier under the rubric of "combat readiness." All concerns of wives and children are ultimately deferred to the necessity of making the soldier ready to desert them. Perhaps this institutionalized infidelity is what makes it so difficult for many women writers to connect the men they love with the men who make war. Few women writers like to see their lovers as killers, and even fewer like to see their lovers weighing their connection so lightly. Even when she supported World War I, Vera Brittain was infuriated that her lover Roland could so automatically place "heroism in the abstract" ahead of their relation in the concrete. And Rebecca West's soldier in *Return of the Soldier* can commit himself to a woman only after he has lost all memory of the war.

The military's conviction that excessive connection to women and children is hostile to its aims is echoed in the academic's conviction that excessive connection to the practical and the personal interferes with his aspirations and obligations. Defending the academic man, and more specifically her Cambridge don husband, F. R. Leavis, Queenie Leavis scoffed at Virginia Woolf's notion in *Three Guineas* of the academic man "hurrying home at four-hour intervals to spend upwards of half an hour giving the baby its bottle."[4] But Woolf insists that the license granted the academic man to forsake the baby and the bottle has led to the vast elaboration not only of the marginalia of literary texts but also of the machinery of war. In a footnote to *Three Guineas*, Woolf meditates on a quotation from *The Report of the Archbishop's Commission on the Ministry of Women*: "At present a married priest is able to fulfil the requirements of the ordination service, 'to forsake and set aside all worldly cares and studies,' largely because his wife can undertake the care of the household and the family . . ." (*The Ministry of Women*, p. 32).

> The Commissioners are here stating and approving a principle which is frequently stated and approved by the dictators. Herr Hitler and Signor Mussolini have both often in very similar words expressed the opinion that "There are two worlds in the life of the nation, the world of men and the world of women"; and proceeded to much the same definition of the duties. The effect which this division has had upon the woman; the petty and personal nature of her interests; her absorption in the practical; her apparent incapacity for the poetical and adventurous—all this has been made the staple of so many novels, the target for so much satire, has confirmed so many theorists in the theory that by the law of nature the woman is less spiritual than the man, that nothing more need be said to prove that she has carried out, willingly or unwillingly, her share of the contract. But very little attention has yet been paid to the intellectual and spiritual effect of this division of duties upon those who are enabled by it "to forsake all worldly cares and studies." Yet there can be no doubt that we owe to this segregation the immense elaboration of modern instruments and methods of war; the astonishing complexities of theology; the vast deposits of notes at the bottom of Greek, Latin and even English texts; the innumerable carvings, chasings and unnecessary ornamentations of our common furniture and crockery; the myriad distinctions of *Debrett* and *Burke*; and all

those meaningless but highly ingenious turnings and twistings into which the intellect ties itself when rid of "the cares of the household and the family." The emphasis which both priests and dictators place upon the necessity for two worlds is enough to prove that it is essential to their domination. (TG 180–81)

Woolf's conviction that the mental liberation from worldly cares and responsibilities enjoyed by the man of letters is as dangerous to the welfare of the human race as is the literal abandonment of wife and family imposed on the soldier by the military, finds expression in many contemporary women writers, most notably Adrienne Rich, Susan Griffin, Assia Djebar, Doris Lessing, and Christa Wolf.

Women's literature on the wars of this century records an increasing recognition of the warmonger in the male intimate: father, husband, lover, brother, mentor, colleague, friend. World War I led Vera Brittain to distrust the glamour of war, but her reservations about war's enthusiasts are undercut by her nostalgia for the intensities of wartime and by her loyalty to the memory of her dead lover, brother, and friends. In a poem recalling Malta, where Brittain was posted as a nurse during the war, the closing lines re-create the haunting beauty of the war years, even though that beauty is asserted to be irrevocably lost.

### We Shall Come No More

So then we came to the Island,
Lissom and young, with the radiant sun in our faces;
Anchored in long quiet lines the ships were waiting,
Giants asleep in the peace of the dark-blue harbour.
Ashore we lept, to seek the magic adventure
Up the valley at noontide,
Where shimmering lay the fields of asphodel.

O *Captain of our Voyage*,
What of the Dead?
Dead days, dead hopes, dead loves, dead dreams, dead sorrows—
O Captain of our Voyage,
Do the dead walk again?

To-day we look for the Island,
Older, a little tired, our confidence waning;
On the ocean bed the shattered ships lie crumbling
Where lost men's bones gleam white in the shrouded silence.
The Island waits, but we shall never find it,
Nor see the dark-blue harbour
Where twilight falls on fields of asphodel. [5]

There is none of Vera Brittain's wistfulness in Sylvia Plath's
response to World War II. No veil of romance obscures the
connection between father and Fascist in "Daddy," and no nostalgia mutes Plath's terror:

You do not do, you do not do
Any more black shoe
In which I have lived like a foot
For thirty years, poor and white,
Barely daring to breathe or Achoo.

. . . . . . . . . . . . . .

I have always been scared of you,
With your Luftwaffe, your gobbledygoo.
And your neat moustache
And your Aryan eye, bright blue.
Panzer-man, panzer-man, O You—

Not God but a swastika
So black no sky could squeak through.
Every woman adores a Fascist,
The boot in the face, the brute
Brute heart of a brute like you. [6]

As father is to daughter, so Nazi is to Jew, so man is to woman. In
"Daddy," the combat zone invades the protected zone of intimate relations between men and women, forcing those relations
to conform to the law of the battlefield.

Toward the end of *The Golden Notebook*, Anna Wulf admits a
similar convergence of the fields of war with the fields of love, but
brings it even closer to home when she recognizes that war has
invaded her and shaped her emotions, so that the logic of her
relation with her lover Saul is the logic of war: "And I knew that

the cruelty and the spite and the I, I, I, I of Saul and Anna were part of the logic of war; and I knew how strong these emotions were, in a way that would never leave me, would become part of how I saw the world."[7] Anna's effort to admit her own cruelty, spite, and egoism, her own participation in the logic that leads to war, is an effort to undermine what she regards as the root cause of war, the imaginative construction of an enemy who bears no resemblance to oneself and who must be overpowered, if not annihilated. Adrienne Rich, in "Trying to Talk with a Man," makes a similar effort at a nuclear testing site when she castigates her husband for "Talking of the danger / as if it were not ourselves / as if we were testing anything else."[8]

The experience of war, in retrospect and in prospect, led Virginia Woolf to hate and fear the English culture and the educated English gentlemen she had loved. Her solution, echoed recently by the Greenham women, was to withdraw from the influence of all patriarchal institutions and of all male intimates, arguing that women could best help men prevent war by being as little like them as possible. By camping next to Cruise missiles, however, the Greenham women forced us to recognize that there is no place to withdraw to, that no spot on earth now lies beyond the arms of educated white men. The separatist solution, while tempting, seems finally to exacerbate the radical separation of the sexes upon which the military and its right hand sciences thrive. The prevention of war would seem to require, on the contrary, the reconstruction of the prevalent form of the relation between the sexes in Western culture, so as to erode the boundaries between male and female, white and black, the abstract and the concrete, the professional and the personal. In a footnote to *Three Guineas*, Woolf notes a promising sign of such reconstruction in the erosion of the identification of manhood with fighting:

> The nature of manhood and the nature of womanhood are frequently defined by both Italian and German dictators. Both repeatedly insist that it is the nature of man and indeed the essence of manhood to fight. Hitler, for example, draws a distinction between "a nation of pacifists and a nation of men." Both repeatedly insist that

it is the nature of womanhood to heal the wounds of the fighter. Nevertheless a very strong movement is on foot towards emancipating man from the old "Natural and eternal law" that man is essentially a fighter; witness the growth of pacifism among the male sex today. . . . It is possible that the Fascist States by revealing to the younger generation at least the need for emancipation from the old conception of virility are doing for the male sex what the Crimean and the European wars did for their sisters. Professor Huxley, however, warns us that "any considerable alteration of the hereditary constitution is an affair of millennia, not of decades." On the other hand, as science also assures us that our life on earth is "an affair of millennia, not of decades," some alteration in the hereditary constitution may be worth attempting. (TG 186–87)

How quickly science changes its tune! Though science no longer assures us that our life on earth is "an affair of millennia," the history of this century (wars, wars, wars, as Sylvia Plath sums it up) insists that we can't rely on short-term solutions alone. And it is in long-term solutions, in "some alteration of the hereditary constitution" as Huxley puts it, in the reconstruction of consciousness as Lessing might put it, that literature plays a crucial role. The last of the romantics and the most rigorous since Shelley, Lessing believes in the power of the imagination to transform human consciousness. By providing what she calls blueprints for alternative constructions of reality, the imagination undermines the determinism of history, biology, and tradition. Lessing's *Marriages between Zones Three, Four, and Five*, the second volume of her *Canopus in Argos* series, is one such blueprint, specifically for altering the prevalent construction of manhood and womanhood in Western culture, a construction that breeds combat between nations and lovers alike.

We enter this narrative confined to the sexually polarized Zones Three and Four. The boundaries between these two zones are closed, and though passage is physically possible from one to the other with protective gear, it occurs to no one in either realm to do so. Represented always by a woman (Al*Ith and then her sister Murti), Zone Three boasts a culture formed to serve and reflect the sexuality of women. As is not uncommon in her realm, Al*Ith is mother to fifty children, some of whom she has borne herself (without pain), more of whom she has adopted but regards as no less, and no more, her own. Every Zone Three child has several parents, gene-father and mind-fathers, gene-mother and mind-mothers, each of whom voluntarily accepts responsibility for the child's rearing and welfare. Monogamy is unthinkable in Zone Three, and Al*Ith's relations with both men and women are as friendly as they are sensual. The boundaries between friend and lover will not, of course, remain clear in a society in which sexuality is identically expressed in the mother's caress and sexual intercourse.

Self-possession is the overriding characteristic of the inhabitants of Zone Three, because coercion is not an option. Al*Ith has no authority, she merely represents her realm and symbolizes its cooperation. Zone Three has no armies, no police, no legal system—no institution that reflects an experience or an expectation of combat. The energies of the inhabitants of Zone Three are released in the making of things, particularly clothes, furniture, and songs. The relation of humans to beasts is equally cooperative in Zone Three, and communication has even been achieved with the trees, some of which are willing and able to act as transmitters of messages between Zone Three citizens.

Lightness, grace, friendliness, composure, content, cooperation, plenty, and emotional ease characterize the atmosphere of Zone Three. In an interview with Minda Berkman in the *New York Times Book Review*, Lessing says she thinks women, left to themselves, are really like this:

> You know, whenever women make imaginary female kingdoms in literature, they are always very permissive, to use the jargon word, and easy and generous and self-indulgent, like the relationships between women when there are no men around. They make each other presents, and they have little feasts, and nobody punishes anyone else. This is the female way of going along when there are no men about or when men are not in the ascendant.[9]

Sharply juxtaposed (so sharply that it nearly kills Al*Ith to cross the border) is Ben Ata's Zone Four. Intensely hierarchical and patriarchal, Zone Four commits all its resources to the army. Though there is no enemy and no war, Zone Four's ideology of combat shapes its cultural and social life. Its architectural monuments are fortresses, its sexuality takes the form of rape, its male children are bred to fight, and its female children are bred to breed fighters. Heaviness, coercion, conflict, scarcity, emotional excess, awkwardness—these are what compose the atmosphere of Zone Four, which Lessing clearly means us to associate with our culture as it is, under the domination of white men.

If the novel stopped here, with the juxtaposition of the two zones, we'd have a relatively familiar feminist critique of patriarchal society, and a relatively familiar feminist fantasy of a matriarchal alternative. We'd have, for example, Marge Piercy's *Woman on the Edge of Time*. But Al*Ith and her zone are jarred into disarray and dismay by the command that Al*Ith marry Ben Ata, that Zone Three have intercourse with Zone Four. Al*Ith greets this command with disgust and repulsion, her perception of Zone Four is like Plath's of Daddy. Ben Ata likes the idea no better, his perception of Zone Three is like Hitler's of pacifists. But the command comes from The Necessity, the name by which inhabitants of both zones know the will of the Canopeans, whose aim is to protect as many species as possible, and who achieve this aim by cross-breeding the more bellicose species with the more nurturant.

As a result of the troubled and painstakingly achieved marriage of Ben Ata and Al*Ith, travel becomes possible not only between Zones Three and Four, but also into the previously unimagined or forgotten Zones Two and Five. Al*Ith receives the knowledge she needs to enter Zone Two from a song originating in Zone Five, and Arusi (the son of Al*Ith and Ben Ata) unites both zones in one body. Zones Three and Four reflect the marriage of their leaders. Ben Ata dismantles his army and sends most of his soldiers home, where they expend their energies in making homes and furniture and rearing their children. He himself is sufficiently reformed to be required to marry Vahshi, the female leader of Zone Five who is now more bellicose than he is. The citizens of Zone Three lose their complacency and recognize that their health and welfare depend not on their ignoring but on their transforming the warmonger at their border. Thus, a novel that begins as a feminist utopia and dystopia, ends with the erosion of the boundary between male and female, with the tempering of both male aggression and female self-enclosure, and with a transformation of duality into multiplicity. The marriage achieved is not the literal marriage of male to female, but the opening of the mind of each to the mind of the other so that each becomes both. Though the metaphor has its origins in an energetically heterosexual and patriarchal culture, its implications are reversed by Lessing when she recommends a marriage in which the battle of the sexes is resolved not between the sexes but in the consciousness of each.

A crucial recognition of women writers of this century who have been able to bear contemplating war and nuclear war, and one clearly embedded in Lessing's conception of Zone Four, is the degree to which the ideology of combat pervades all our institutions, shaping to its assumptions our most private, as well as our most public, experiences. If women, as Woolf suggests in *A Room of One's Own*, were so shocked in August 1914 "to see the faces of our rulers in the light of the shell-fire"[10] that romance was killed, the light of the shell-fire since has steadily killed our faith in the liberal education of our rulers as well. When Woolf asks a decade later, in 1938, "Where is it leading us, the procession of educated men?" she answers, emphatically and repeatedly, to war. Woolf goes on to argue in *Three Guineas* that the patriarchal structure of the home and of the professions encourages the bellicosity that leads to war, making men "possessive, jealous of any infringement of their rights, and highly combative if anyone dares dispute them" (*TG* 66). In "Toward a Woman-Centered University" written forty years later, Adrienne Rich insists that combativeness remains the dominant note of higher education in America. Quoting at length from Leonard Kriegel's critique of his graduate education at Columbia, Rich points out that certain terms in the above quotation have a familiar ring: defending, attacking, combat, status, banking, dueled, power, making it. They suggest the connections—actual and metaphoric—between the style of the university and the style of a society invested in military and economic aggression. In each of these accounts what stands out is not the passion for "learning for its own sake" or the sense of an intellectual community, but the dominance of the masculine ideal, the race of men against one another, the conversion of an end to a means.[11]

One thing the three major social movements of the sixties— the Civil Rights Movement, the Antiwar Movement, and the Feminist Movement—had in common was a critique of the cultural presumptuousness of white American men, and this critique has had some lasting impact on literary studies in this country. Covering the meeting of the Modern Language Association in San Francisco in December 1987, Joseph Berger of the *New York Times* comes to the conclusion that the crucial issue under debate in American academic literary circles is, Can we know what literature is superior? Twenty years ago, the superiority of literature by white men was assumed at the MLA, so this debate does point to a certain erosion, in the last two decades, of the white American male academic's assurance of his cultural preeminence, a certain unhinging of his easy confidence in the "superior spiritual status" of his kind. But note with what bellicosity the idea of an alternate, an alien body of literature, is entertained at the MLA. "U.S. Literature: Canon Under Siege," Berger titles his article, and who can fail to hear the echoes of Khe Sanh, who can fail to see, particularly if she has been reading a good many Vietnam novels, the beleaguered white man's books—the best he's seen and thought and done—dragged down into the animal mud of books by women and African Americans and Native Americans and Asians and what have you. Though drenched in a sentiment we owe in part to our literary representations of Vietnam, the sentiment that allows white American men to perceive themselves as victims of the tragedies their assumption of superiority creates, the article does document an increasing tolerance in academic circles for literature by authors who are not white men. Though remnants of the conviction that the best that has been seen, thought, and done by white men is all we need know surface in the remarks of several prominent literary critics who variously mourn the loss of "once-honored standards like grace of style, vigor of prose and originality of expression,"[12] the article points out that this position is under fire and losing ground. We are no longer quite so convinced that the white man's literature is the only one we need know, or that it does indeed embody the best that has been seen and thought and done. In fact, as Berger points out, a good deal of work is currently being done on how literary reputations are constructed, on how networks of white men in criticism, academics, and publishing engineer the canonization of writers of their circle.

Though the MLA seems prepared to make a little room for a number of literatures it once dismissed as "popular" or "available only in translation," and though the MLA seems prepared, even, to allow that "the New England spinster['s] struggl[e] to 'grow old with dignity'" is as much a paradigm of heroism as the matador's performance in the bull ring (USL), the MLA shows no inclination to launch a serious critique of the canon of Western literature as enshrining the cultural values of a race and a sex with a formidable history of violence. Its intention is to assimilate other literatures and other cultures, not to transform its own. The premise of Lessing's *Marriage between Zones Three, Four, and Five* is not just that we need to be familiar with other cultures, but also that we need to discover in other cultures less pugnacious ways of structuring our feelings, of structuring our whole apprehension of life.

That this is a lesson we have yet to learn was brought home to me by an article in the *New York Times Magazine* (February 9, 1986), entitled "The Tyranny of the Yale Critics," which featured stunning portraits of Jacques Derrida in a designer overcoat leaning pensively at twilight against a stone pillar, Harold Bloom sinking ponderously into his leather lounge chair amid a sea of papers and books, Geoffrey Hartman in a prophet's white beard aspiring to the stained glass window behind him, and J. Hillis

Miller nattily dressed looking up from his book at the Naples
Pizza Parlor in New Haven. These well-upholstered men at the
top of their profession have, of course, their quarrels with each
other but none has any quarrel with his position. They practice a
form of literary criticism known as deconstruction. In an effort to
rescue his critical method from the belligerent implications of its
name, J. Hillis Miller argues that deconstruction is not "demoli-
tion" of the text. Rather,

> such criticism is an activity turning something unified back to de-
> tached fragments or parts. It suggests the image of a child taking apart
> his father's watch, reducing it back to useless parts, beyond any
> reconstruction. A deconstructionalist is not a parasite but a par-
> ricide. He is a bad son demolishing beyond hope of repair the
> machine of Western metaphysics. [13]

The mollifying image of the child taking apart *his* father's watch
obscures neither the male-centeredness nor the aggressiveness of
this parricidal approach to literary texts. However much we may
wish to see the machine of Western metaphysics dismantled, we
will not do so through the militarist language or the elitist practices of the Yale critics.

"The university is above all a hierarchy," Rich writes in "Toward a Woman-Centered University":

> At the top is a small cluster of highly paid and prestigious persons,
> chiefly men, whose careers entail the services of a very large base of
> ill-paid or unpaid persons, chiefly women: wives, research assistants,
> secretaries, teaching assistants, cleaning women, waitresses in the
> faculty club, lower-echelon administrators, and women students
> who are used in various ways to gratify the ego. (*OLSS* 136)

Though we don't see in the *Times*'s portraits of the Yale critics the
bevy of ill-paid women behind them, if we followed the accounts
of the painful efforts of clerical workers at Yale to augment their
pitifully small salaries, we will know they are there. If we are to
take seriously Woolf's advice that women can best prevent war by
being as little like men as possible, it follows that our institutions
of higher learning must not just accommodate women but reflect
whatever it is in the lives and habits of women that tempers their

bellicosity and their presumptuousness. This means not just adding a bathroom here and a woman faculty member there, but modeling the content, structure, and language of education after the lives of women. In recent years, for example, the university has grudgingly accepted some responsibility for child care, but only to release women from time to time from their children so that they can be more easily accommodated in male-devised structures that cannot function in the presence of children. No institution of higher learning requires, or even encourages, *all* its faculty to participate in the care of children, and few regard discourse addressed to children as a serious intellectual undertaking. Women have spent a good deal of time with children, learning how to communicate across a great divide in knowledge and understanding, how to live with irrationality, how to curb the impulse to use brute force—lessons surely useful to the prevention of war. Women's lives have centered in making and caring for things at home and in the community, in living and working with family and neighbors, in reading and writing and painting and playing musical instruments not as a means to prestige or riches or position, but for their own sake—activities surely useful to the prevention of war. And women have cultivated the mother tongue, a language used to communicate rather than to perplex or exclude, and a language richly and determinedly attached to the actual. A university sincerely interested in preventing war would insist on the connection between these activities and "higher" thought rather than impose a dichotomy between them. As Grace Paley puts it in an article in *Resist*, "I just don't believe in armed struggle as a way to change the world, or the neighborhood."

"I was never ready to be less than wary about the relations between tutors and taught," Johor reminds us in *Shikasta*. In these days of what Cynthia Enloe calls "militarized peacetime," of the battle of the deconstructionists and the reconstructionists, the battle of the sexes, race war, Cold War, terrorism, and blatant U.S. provocation in Central America and the Middle East, in these days of super bowls and presidential campaigns waged on the principle that winning is the only thing, we might do well to consider why we have failed to be sufficiently wary not only of the military and the military sciences, but also of what we like to call liberal education. "To fight has always been the man's habit, not the woman's," Woolf points out in *Three Guineas*, and as long as our memory of war is constructed by soldiers and our higher education consists overwhelmingly of books by white men taught by white men, to fight will be the habit of our culture.

## NOTES

1. Virginia Woolf, *Three Guineas* (New York, 1938), 87–88. Hereafter referred to as *TG*.
2. William Broyles, Jr., "Why Men Love War," *Esquire*, November 1984, 61.
3. Quentin Bell, *Virginia Woolf: A Biography* (New York, 1972), 205.
4. Queenie Leavis, "Caterpillars of the World Unite," in *The Importance of Scrutiny*, ed. Eric Bentley (New York, 1948), 389.
5. Vera Brittain, *Testament of Youth* (New York, 1980), 290.
6. Sylvia Plath, *Ariel* (New York, 1965), 49–50.
7. Doris Lessing, *The Golden Notebook* (New York, 1973), 589.
8. Adrienne Rich, *Diving into the Wreck* (New York, 1973), 4.
9. Minda Berkman, "A Talk With Doris Lessing," *New York Times Book Review*, March 30, 1980, 24.
10. Virginia Woolf, *A Room of One's Own* (New York, 1929), 15.
11. Adrienne Rich, *On Lies, Secrets, and Silence* (New York, 1979), 129–30. Hereafter referred to as *OLSS*.
12. Joseph Berger, "U.S. Literature: Canon Under Siege," *New York Times*, January 6, 1988. Hereafter referred to as *USL*.
13. Colin Campbell, "The Tyranny of the Yale Critics," *New York Times Magazine*, February 9, 1986, 25.

## Planting Tulips

**I**f the day were mid-fall, October say, sunny and clear as brook water, you might see her barefoot in Levi's, her sweater as orange as that maple next door. She'd be straining like a mule, hauling a bag of peat moss from the garage to the stone wall between her yard and the orchard. If you paused and looked again, you might catch her stepping more lightly, a bag of bone meal in one hand, a shovel over her shoulder as if she means to dig to China. She'll make yet another trip to the garage for gardening gloves, a trowel, and tulip bulbs in a brown paper bag she carries out in front of her like a child her lunch to school. And if you now silently wait, you will see her stoop. Her tools and materials clustered in a broken ring around her, she will bend and study the earth. You will not be discovered, she sees only tulips now, Peerless Pinks under the dogwood tree, Golden Melodies near the azalea, Orange Emperors where the rose bush used to be. As her eyes flicker among these three precisely defined places, you may think her thoughts must be elsewhere, so pensively, so statuesquely does she stoop, chin poised on elbow poised on up-raised knee, the eyes alone alive.

If you read a lot, you who are watching now, you will perhaps prefer to any place on earth (to this place where you stand now watching a woman plant tulip bulbs, to those three places she interchanges her tulips so lovingly among), a spot upstairs in your house where your old Morris chair still cradles the book you put aside to go for your walk. It will occur to you, then, that this woman recalls Ceres's tender preparations for her daughter's winter burial. She plants her tulips, you will say to yourself, to revive the ancient wisdom of the mothers, that we die in the service of life. And you will not be surprised when her head juts up and the pure clear curve of her back cracks into sharp planes of motion. When her shovel thrusts rudely at the roots of the dogwood, overturning a massive clod of earth, you will not be uneasy when she smashes it to smithereens. You will know this angularity of motion expresses a necessary violence. The earth will recover. The daughter, too, you will remember, will revive in the spring, you can see her in your mind's eye, radiant, death's kingdom behind her, a blood-red poppy in her hair.

But perhaps you do not read, you who are so still and watch this woman so intently, perhaps your eyes have failed you and what you see now in that yard over there is someone walking, someone bending, someone digging. It is a woman? Is she burying something? Has a cat, a rabbit, a canary died? And you remember your first cemetery under a rhododendron bush, and your heart-shaped locket sacrificed to a dead bird. And you remember all the cemeteries since—Arlington National Cemetery, the National Memorial Cemetery of the Pacific, the wall in Washington because there weren't any remains of your grandson—and you only wish you could collect all your dead in one place, under that maple over there perhaps, as orange as that woman's sweater.

But why so funereal, you ask, why should she give her bounty to the dead? You are a young woman, sharp-eyed, sharp-tongued, irked to find you've taken a moment from your busy day to watch this woman plant tulip bulbs. A housewife, you mutter, time on her hands. And you are amazed at how slowly she works. Three trips to the garage, you could have done it in two, and then all that staring at the ground. You would just plunge in and dig. And you feel released when the woman hacks with her shovel at the roots of the dogwood, you are glad when she smashes the clod, you see that she clears

ground, makes her mark. A woman scoring the earth contents
you and you walk away briskly, whistling perhaps, serene in the
mark you make on the earth.

Her clothes deceive you and you take her for a younger
woman, a daughter of the earth, and you celebrate her work.
You appreciate the sway of her hips as she hauls peat moss,
you grin at the jaunty way she carries her shovel, you think her
too bashful to raise her eyes to you when she lowers them to
the soil. And when she digs, an illusion is shattered, she isn't
thinking of you after all, she's thinking of the dirt and the
flowers she wants to grow, and you blame her for being older
than you thought and unworthy of your notice.

You see it as magic, as you see all your mother's work. How
does she know about the peat moss, the bone meal, how does
she know how deep to dip the holes? And you help the only
way you know how, you spin the names of tulips in an incanta-
tion all your own:

> Peerless Pink, lovely I think
> Golden Melody, like a bumblebee
> Orange Emperor, have you anymore?

And in the spring if the tulips blossom, you will have forgotten
their planting, and you will think them the work of the stars,
the sun, the moon.